KNITTING EMPORIUM

A collection of designs
for hand knitting by
JO SHARP

The Taunton Press

Published by
Jo Sharp Pty Ltd
A. C. N. 056 596 439
P.O. Box 357
Albany WA 6331, Australia
www.josharp.com.au
email: yarn@josharp.com.au

Printed in Australia

The Taunton Press, Inc.
63 South Main Street
P.O. Box 5506
Newtown, CT 06470-5506
www.taunton.com
email: tp@taunton.com

Taunton
BOOKS & VIDEOS
for fellow enthusiasts

Distributed by Publishers Group West

ISBN 1-56158-443-6

Acknowledgments

Creative Director *Jo Sharp*
Garment Design *Jo Sharp, Leanne Prouse.*
Knitting *Norma Beard, Janet Best, Wendy Carmen, Sonia Charewicz, Lyn Charlesworth, Margaret Cusick, Janice Darrah, Helena Dehaan, Lily De Roost, Francesca Greaves, Jenny Green, Carolyne Greeney, Betty Hawkins, Hazel Heggie, Klaudia Krajnc, Sheila Min, Sylvia Ovens, Leanne Prouse, Marilyn Theisel*
Photography *Jo Sharp, Andrew Markovs.*
Portraits of Jo Sharp *Lisa Thompson*
Photography Styling & Assistants *Wendy Richards, Leanne Prouse*
Models *Peter Robertson, Renay Simmons / Vivien's Model Management*
Hair *Hot Lox Salon*
Location credits *Cellos of Churchlane*
Film Processing *Rainbow Pro Photo Lab*
Book Design *Stumpfel Shaw, Jo Sharp Pty Ltd*
Poem *Jo Sharp*
Diagrams *Bronia Richards*
Knitting Graphs *Stitch Painter Gold*
Computer Consultant *Scott Parsons*
Printing Preparation *CDC Graphics & Multi Colour*
Printing *Frank Daniels Pty Ltd*

CONTENTS

KNITTING EMPORIUM

Millefiori fields

where Balthazar played

Whispering colours

of Kashmir, Tashkent, Oriole

and heathery dusk

till winter solstice late

Tip toeing down the river bed

shallow and bespangled

Arabella found a mirage

of some antipodean land

That wonderous night

watched by the stellar eclipse

Christobel and Anastasia

in the light

Tension

At the start of each pattern, the required tension is given. Before beginning, it is most important that you knit a tension square. Using the stitch and needles specified in pattern, cast on 40 sts and knit approx. 40 rows. Lay work flat and without stretching, measure 10cm both vertically and horizontally with a ruler. Mark with pins. Count the stitches and rows in between the pins, these should match the required tension. If not, you will need to change needle size. Smaller needles will bring the stitches closer together, larger needles will spread the stitches out. Incorrect tension will result in a mis-shapen garment.

It sometimes occurs that while the stitch tension given in a pattern can be achieved, the row tension is incorrect. In this case, work the rows required to achieve the length specified in the diagram, rather than working to the number of rows specified in pattern. This is easily achieved on sections of work where no shaping is involved, however where shaping is involved, calculations will be necessary in order to produce similar shaping at the required length.
In particular, if the arm hole rows on a fully shaped garment are reduced to achieve correct armhole depth, shaping rows on the sleeve top will also need to be altered.

Sizing

The bodice circumference measurements given for each pattern are calculated after a 2cm seam allowance has been deducted. Bodice diagram measurements have no seam allowance deducted. To ascertain which size garment to knit, use as a guide, a favourite old sweater which fits the intended wearer well. Compare the measurements of this garment with the measurements given in the pattern diagram and choose the size which most closely matches the existing garment.

Note that some patterns are designed to fit snugly, whilst others are loose fitting.

Yarn quantities

Quantities of yarn are based on average requirements using specified tension and Jo Sharp 8ply DK Pure Wool Hand Knitting Yarn. Responsibility cannot be accepted for finished garment if substitute yarns are used.

Graphs

Each square on a graph represents one stitch. Unless otherwise stated, graphs are worked in Stocking Stitch. When working from a graph, read odd rows (RS) from right to left and even rows (WS) from left to right. Each colour used on the graph is shown by a symbol or number which is notated in the Key of the pattern being knitted.

Graphs may be enlarged by photocopier, for easier reading.

Colour reproduction

Inaccuracies of some illustrated yarn shades in this book are caused by photographic and printing reproduction processes and are unavoidable. To avoid disappointment, it is advisable to refer to a Jo Sharp Yarn Sample Card to view actual yarn shades (see page 101) specified in patterns before purchasing yarn.

Knitting Jo Sharp garments for re-sale

The Knitting of garments from this book for re-sale is not permitted without written permission from Jo Sharp Pty Ltd, address as below.

Pattern queries

Write to:
Jo Sharp Pty Ltd
PO Box 357 Albany 6331
Western Australia
email: yarn@josharp.com.au
www.josharp.com.au

ABBREVIATIONS

alt	alternate
approx.	approximately
beg	beginning
cm	centimetre
col	colour
cont	continue
cn	cable needle
dec	decrease
dia	diameter
foll	follow/ing/s
inc	increase
incl.	inclusive
k	knit
kb1	knit into back of next st.
M1	make one - pick up loop between sts and K into back of it
mm	millimetre
p	purl
patt	pattern
Pb1	purl into back of next st.
psso	pass slipped stitch over
rem	remain/ing/der
rep	repeat
rev	reverse/ing
RS	right side
Sl	slip
st/s	stitch/es
st st	stocking stitch
tbl	through back of loop
tog	together
WS	wrong side
yb	yarn back
yf	yarn forward
yon	yarn over needle
yrn	yarn around needle

MEASUREMENTS

Sizes	A	(B	C)	
To fit bust	80	90	100	cm
Bodice circumference	83	93	103	cm
Bodice length	54	54	55	cm
Sleeve seam (long)	43	43	43	cm
Sleeve seam (short)	6	8	8	cm

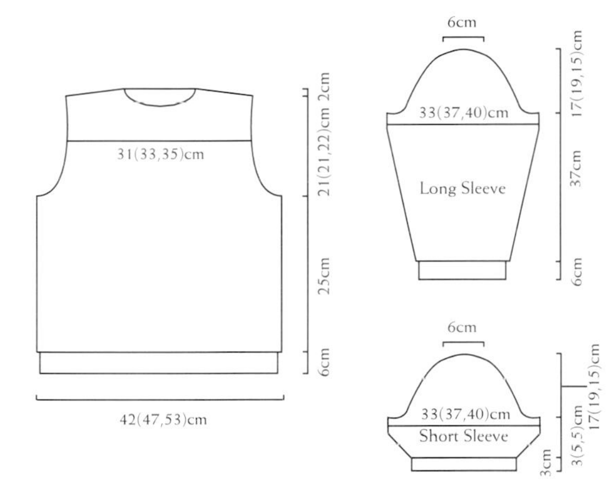

YARN

Jo Sharp 8 ply DK Pure Wool Hand Knitting Yarn

Code	Colour	Yarn Quantity			
Sizes		A	(B	C)	
Sweater with short sleeve (previous 2 pages)					
A	Summer 001	4	4	5	x 50g balls
B	Winter 904	5	5	5	x 50g balls
Sweater with long sleeve (left & right)					
A	Winter 904	5	5	5	x 50g balls
B	Heron 802	5	5	6	x 50g balls

NEEDLES

1 pair 3.25mm needles (USA 3) (UK 10)
1 pair 4.00mm needles (USA 6) (UK 8)
1 set 3.25mm circular needles (USA 3) (UK 10)

Christobel - long sleeve version, left & above
Christobel - short sleeve version, previous 2 pages

TENSION

22.5 sts and 30 rows measured over 10cm (approx. 4") of Stocking Stitch using 4.00mm needles.

COLOUR SEQUENCE

Work 10 rows col A, then 10 rows col B.
Rep these 20 rows throughout

BACK

Using 3.25mm needles and col B, cast on 95(107,119)sts. Work 18 rows k1, p1 rib. Change to 4.00mm needles and following Colour Sequence, work 74 rows st st (25cm, excluding band).

Shape armholes (RS) Cast off 6(8,10)sts at beg of next 2 rows. Dec 1 st at each end of next row, then foll alt rows 5(7,9)times [71(75,79)sts] [87(91,95)rows] **

Work 49(45,45)rows without shaping. [136(136,140)rows] [45(45,46)cm excluding band].

Shape shoulders (RS) Cast off 7(7,8)sts at beg of next 4 rows, then 8(9,8)sts at beg of foll 2 rows. Cast off rem 27(29,31)sts.

FRONT

Work as for back to **.

Work 29(23,21)rows [116(114,116)rows] [39(38,39)cm, excluding band].

Shape neck Row 1 (RS) Work 28(30,32)sts, turn and leave rem 43(45,47)sts on a holder. Work each side of neck separately.

Dec 1 st at neck edge in every alt row 6(7,8)times [22(23,24)sts] [129(129,133)rows]. Work 7 rows without shaping.

Shape shoulder Cast off 7(7,8)sts at beg of next row and foll alt rows. Work 1 row. Cast off rem 8(9,8)sts. Slip next 15 sts on to stitch holder. Join yarn to rem sts and work second side to match first side, reversing all shaping.

SLEEVES

For long sleeve version only.

Using 3.25mm needles and col A, cast on 47(49,49)sts and work 20 rows in k1, p1 rib.
Change to 4.00mm needles and working in Colour Sequence, beg with col B, work 4 rows without shaping.
Shape sleeve Keeping colour sequence correct, inc 1 st at each end of next row, then every 4th row, 2(5,17)times, then every 6th row 11(11,3)times [75(83,91)sts].
Cont in patt without shaping until work measures 43cm (including band) and ending on a WS row.

For short sleeve version only

Using 3.25mm needles and col A, cast on 66(70,78)sts and work 3cm in k1, p1 rib increasing 5 sts evenly across last WS row [71(75,83)sts].
Change to 4.00mm needles and working in Colour Sequence, beg with col A, work 1 row.
Shape Sleeve Inc 1 st at each end of next row, then every foll 3rd row 1(3,3)times [75(83,91)sts]. Work 5(3,5)rows without shaping.

For both versions.

Shape sleeve top (RS) Cast off 3(3,4)sts at beg of next 2 rows. Now dec 1 st at each end of next row, then every alt row 12(10,9)times, then every row 15(21,25)times (13sts)
[42(44,46)sleeve top shaping rows].

MAKING UP

Press all pieces gently on WS using a warm iron over a damp cloth. Using Backstitch, join shoulder seams. Centre sleeves and join. Join side and sleeve seams using Edge to Edge stitch on ribs.
With RS facing using 3.25mm circular needles and col B, pick up and knit 24(26,28)sts down left front neck, 15sts from holder at centre front, 24(26,28)sts up right front neck and 27(29,31)sts across back neck [90(96,102)sts].
Work in rounds of k1, p1 rib until neckband measures 4cm.
Change to 4.00mm needles and cont until band measures 8.5cm. Cast off in rib. Press seams.

Christobel - long sleeve version, above
Christobel - short sleeve version, right

SOLSTICE

MEASUREMENTS

Sizes	A	(B	C	D)	
To fit Bust	80	90	100	110	cm
Bodice Circumference	114	120	126	130	cm
Bodice Length	64	66	68	70	cm
Sleeve Length	42	42	44	44	cm

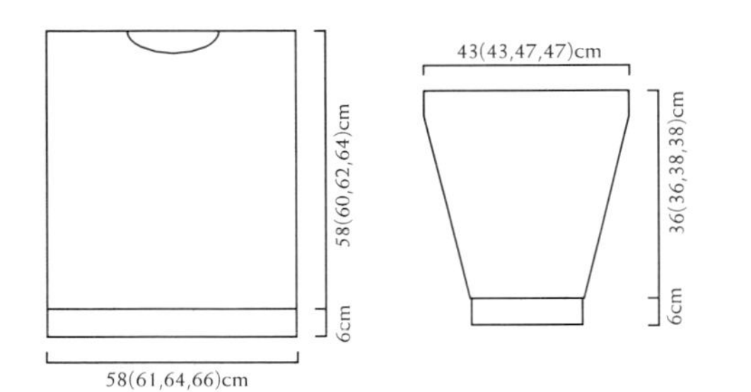

YARN

Jo Sharp 8 ply DK Pure Wool Hand Knitting Yarn

Code	Colour	Yarn Quantity				
Sizes		A	(B	C	D)	
Women's Sweater Version 1 (left)						
A	Orchard 906	2	2	2	2	x 50g balls
B	Lilac 324	3	3	4	4	x 50g balls
C	Mulberry 325	3	4	4	4	x 50g balls
D	Heron 802	2	3	3	3	x 50g balls
E	Violet 319	2	2	2	3	x 50g balls
F	Storm 706	2	2	2	3	x 50g balls
G	Ink 901	2	3	3	3	x 50g balls
Women's Sweater Version 2 (previous 2 pages and top right)						
A	Smoke 339	2	3	3	3	x 50g balls
B	Ruby 326	3	3	4	4	x 50g balls
C	Tangerine 003	2	3	3	3	x 50g balls
D	Aegean 504	2	3	3	3	x 50g balls
E	Chartreuse 330	2	2	2	3	x 50g balls
F	Wine 307	2	2	2	3	x 50g balls
G	Owl 801	2	3	3	3	x 50g balls

NEEDLES

1 pair 3.75mm (USA 5) (UK 9)
1 pair 4.00mm (USA 6) (UK 8)
1 set 3.75mm circular needles (USA 5) (UK 9)

Solstice - Version 1, left
Solstice - Version 2, previous 2 pages and top right

TENSION

22sts and 30 rows to 10cm (approx. 4") measured over Texture Pattern using 4.00mm needles.

TEXTURE PATTERN

Multiple 4 + 3

Special abbreviations

wyif - with yarn in front
wyib - with yarn in back

Note; Slip all slip stitches purlwise.

Working in stocking stitch;

Row 1 & 2 col A.
Row 3 col B.
Rows 4 - 6 col C.
Row 7 col D, P3 *k1, p3; rep from * to end.
Row 8 col E, Purl.
Now working in st st
Row 9 - 11 col C.
Row 12 col B.
Rows 13 & 14 col A.
Row 15 & 16 col F.
Row 17 col E, K3 *wyib sl1, k3; rep from * to end.
Row 18 col E, K3 *wyif sl1, k3; rep from * to end.
Row 19 col C, K1 * wyib sl1, k3; rep from * to last sl1, k1.
Row 20 col C, K1 *wyif sl1, k3; rep from * to last sl1, k1.
Row 21 col D, Rep row 17.
Row 22 col D, P1, k1, p1, * wyif sl1, p1, k1, p1; rep from * to end.
Now working in st st
Rows 23 & 24 col F.

Rows 25 & 26 col G.
Row 27 col C.
Rows 28 - 30 col B.
Row 31 col A, as row 7.
Row 32 col E, Purl.
Now working in st st;
Rows 33 - 35 col B.
Row 36 col C.
Rows 37 & 38 col G.
Row 39 & 40 col D.
Row 41 col F, as row 17.
Row 42 col F, as row 18.
Row 43 col E, as row 19.
Row 44 col E, as row 20.
Row 45 col B, as row 17.
Row 46 col B, as row 22.
Row 47 col D, Knit.
Row 48 col D, Purl.
Rows 1 - 48 form pattern repeat.

FRONT

Using 3.75mm needles and (col C for version 1 or col A for version 2), cast on 132(138,144,150)sts.
Row 1 (RS) * K3, k1, p1, k1; rep from * to end.
Row 2 * K1, p1, k1, p3; rep from * to end.
These 2 rows form rib pattern.
In row 3, change to col G and cont until work measures 6cm, increasing 1 st on last WS row [133(139,145,151)sts].
Change to 4.00mm needles and work 51(53,55,57)cm, excluding band, in Texture Pattern repeat, ending on a WS row.
Shape neck Work 54(57,60,63)sts, turn and leave rem sts on holder. Work each side of neck separately. Cast off 2 sts at neck edge on next row, then foll alt rows, twice, then 1 st on foll alt rows, 3 times [45(48,51,54)sts]. Work 10 rows without shaping. Cast off.
With RS facing, leave 25 sts on a holder, rejoin yarn to rem sts and work second side to match first side, reversing all shaping.

BACK

Work Back Bodice to match Front Bodice, omitting neck shaping.

SLEEVES

Using 3.75mm needles and (col C for version 1 or col A for version 2) cast on 48(48,54,54)sts.
Row 1 (RS) * K3, k1, p1, k1; rep from * to end.
Row 2 * K1, p1, k1, p3; rep from * to end.
These 2 rows form pattern.
In row 3, change to col G and cont until work measures 6cm, increasing 15(15,13,13)sts evenly across last WS row 63(63,67,67)sts.
Change to 4.00mm needles and working in Texture Pattern repeat, shape sleeve as follows;
Inc 1 st at each end of foll 6th row, 17(17,10,10)times, then every foll 5th row, 0(0,10,10)times [97(97,107,107)sts] [102(102,110,110)shaping rows].
Work 6(6,4,4)rows without shaping. Adjust length here if desired. Cast off.

MAKING UP

Press all pieces (except ribs) gently on WS using a warm iron over a damp cloth. Using Backstitch join shoulder seams. Centre sleeves and join, join side and sleeve seams.
Neckband Using 3.75mm circular needle and (col C, version 1 or A, version 2) with RS facing, pick up and knit 28 sts down left front neck, 25 sts from holder at centre, 28 sts up right front and 45 sts across back neck (126 sts).
Round 1 * K3, k1, p1, k1; rep from * to end.
Round 2 * K3, p1, k1, p1; rep from * to end.
These 2 rounds form pattern.
In round 3, change to col G and work a further 12 rounds, change to (col C, Version 1 or col A, Version 2). Patt 3 rounds. Cast off knit sts in knit and Moss sts in purl. Press seams.

Solstice - Version 1, right

ANTIPODEAN

MEASUREMENT

Unisex Sizes	A	(B	C	D)	
To fit chest/bust	80-90	90-100	100-110	110-120	cm
Bodice circumference	110	120	130	140	cm
Bodice length	62	63	65	67	cm
Sleeve length	44	44	51	51	cm

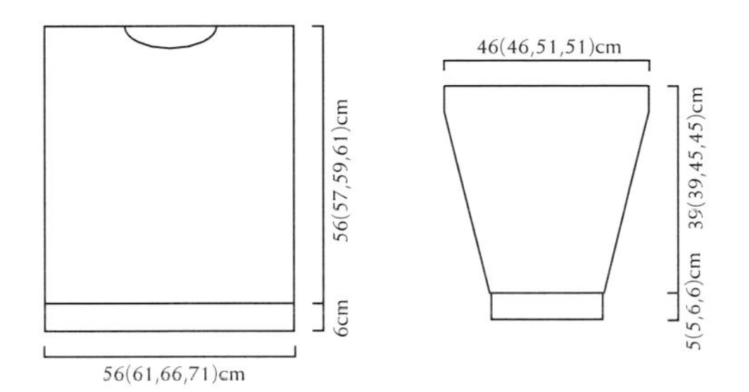

YARN

Jo Sharp 8 ply DK Pure Wool Hand Knitting Yarn

Colour	Yarn Quantity				
Unisex Sizes	A	(B	C	D)	
Women's Version					
Tangerine 003	13	14	15	16	x 50 g balls
Men's Version					
Navy 327	14	15	15	16	x 50 g balls

NEEDLES

1 pair 3.75mm (USA 5) (UK 9)
1 pair 4.50mm (USA 7) (UK 7)
1 set 3.75mm circular needles (USA 5) (UK 9)

TENSION

19.5 sts and 26 rows measured over 10cm (approx 4") of Stocking Stitch using 4.50mm needles.

FRONT

Using 4.50 mm needles, cast on 110(120,130,140)sts
Row 1 (RS) P2, k3 to end.
Row 2 P3, k2 to end.
Repeat rows 1 & 2 until rib measures 6cm.
Now work 51(52,54,56)cm st st, ending on a WS row [57(58,60,62)cm, including band]
Shape neck Work 44(49,53,58)sts, turn and leave rem 66(71,77,82)sts on a holder. Work each side of neck separately. Cast off 3 sts at beg of next row, then 3 sts at neck edge on foll alt rows, 3 times. Then dec 1 st at beg of next alt row.

Antipodean - Women's sweater, left
Antipodean - Men's Sweater, previous 2 pages

Shape shoulder (RS) Cast off 10(12,13,14)sts at beg of next row and foll alt row. Work 1 row. Cast off rem 11(12,14,17)sts.
With RS facing, leave 22(22,24,24)sts on holder, rejoin yarn to rem sts and complete second side to match first side, rev all shaping.

BACK

Work back to match front, incorporating shoulder shaping on the last 6 rows as follows;
(RS) Cast off 10(12,13,14)sts at beg of next 4 rows, then 11(12,14,16)sts at beg of next 2 rows. Cast off rem 48(48,50,52)sts.

SLEEVES

It is advised, when knitting this unisex garment for a man in size A, B, C or D, to use size C or D sleeve.
Using 3.75mm needles, cast on 50(50,60,60)sts and work 16(16,18,18)rows rib as for Front, increasing 10 sts in last WS row [60(60,70,70)sts].
Change to 4.50mm needles and work 12 rows st st.
Shape sleeve Cont in st st AT THE SAME TIME inc 1 st at each end of next row then every foll 3rd row 13 times, then every foll 3rd(3rd,5th,5th)row, 4 times [96(96,106,106)sts] [80(80,90,90)rows, including band]. Work a further 35(35,44,44)rows without shaping, or until length desired. Cast off.

MAKING UP

Press all pieces, except ribbing, gently on WS using a warm iron over a damp cloth. Using Backstitch, join shoulder seams. Centre sleeves and join, join side and sleeve seams using Edge to Edge stitch on ribs.
Neckband *For Women's Version only*
With RS facing, using 3.75mm circular needles, pick up and k 25 sts down left side front neck, 22(22,26,26)sts from st holder at centre front, 25 sts up right side front neck and 48(48,49,49)sts across back neck [120(120,125,125)sts].
Round 1 *K4, p1; rep from * to end.
Continue in rounds as set until neck band measures 12 cm, cast off in rib. Fold collar to inside and sew in place. Press seams.
Neckband for Men's Version only
With RS facing, using 3.75mm circular needles, pick up and k 25 sts down left side front neck, 22(22,26,26)sts from st holder at centre front, 25 sts up right side front neck and 48(48,50,50)sts across back neck [120(120,126,126)sts]. Work in rounds of k2, p2 rib, until collar measures 7cm.
Cast off in rib. Press seams.

TASHKENT

MEASUREMENTS

Hat Sizes	One Size fits all				
Cardigan Sizes	A	(B	C	D)	
To fit bust	80	90	100	110	cm
Bodice circumference	101	110	119	128	cm
Bodice length	61	61	64	64	cm
Sleeve length	45	45	45	45	cm

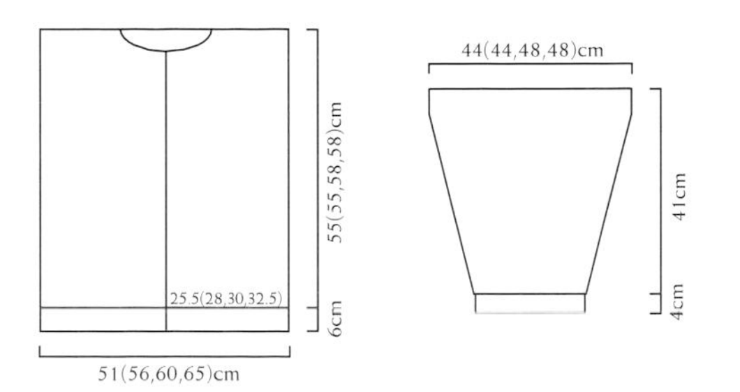

Code	Key	Colour	Yarn Quantity A	(B	C	D)	
Cardgian Version 1 (left)							
	□	Mulberry 325	2	2	2	2	x 50g balls
	■	Ebony 902	2	2	2	2	x 50g balls
A	☒	Slate 328	4	5	5	5	x 50g balls
C	◇	Wine 307	3	3	3	3	x 50g balls
	+	Amethyst 503	3	3	3	3	x 50g balls
	O	Chestnut 506	1	1	1	1	x 50g ball
	∩	Khaki 329	1	1	1	1	x 50g ball
	♥	Brick 333	2	2	2	2	x 50g balls
	I	Lilac 324	1	2	2	2	x 50g balls
	−	Chartreuse 330	1	1	1	1	x 50g ball
	⧅	Miro 507	2	2	2	2	x 50g balls
	◢	Gold 320	1	2	2	2	x 50g balls
	∪	Olive 313	1	1	1	1	x 50g ball
B	▪	Ginger 322	1	1	1	1	x 50g ball
	✣	Antique 323	1	1	1	1	x 50g ball
	⧄	Khaki 329	(yarn allocated above)				
Cardigan Version 2 (previous 4 pages)							
	□	Amethyst 503	2	2	2	2	x 50g balls
A	■	Navy 327	6	6	6	6	x 50g balls
B	☒	Miro 507	4	5	5	5	x 50g balls
C	◇	Owl 801	4	4	4	4	x 50g balls
	+	Navy 327	(yarn allocated above)				
	O	Ink 901	1	1	1	1	x 50g ball
	∩	Navy 327	(yarn allocated above)				
	♥	Mulberry 325	2	2	2	2	x 50g balls
	I	Linen 335	1	2	2	2	x 50g balls
	−	Chartreuse 330	1	1	1	1	x 50g ball
	⧅	Forest 318	2	2	2	2	x 50g balls
	◢	Antique 323	1	2	2	2	x 50g balls
	∪	Cape 508	1	1	1	1	x 50g ball
	▪	Lilac 324	1	1	1	1	x 50g ball
	✣	Jade 316	1	1	1	1	x 50g ball
	⧄	Owl 801	(yarn allocated above)				

Tashkent - Version 1, left
Tashkent - Version 2, previous 4 pages

YARN

Jo Sharp 8ply DK Pure Wool Hand Knitting Yarn

Hat - Version 1, left

Note. The book cover version of this hat does not show a contrasting colour on the crown.

A	Slate 328	1 x 50g ball
B	Owl 801	1 x 50g ball

Hat - Version 2, previous 4 pages

Storm 706 — 1 x 50g ball

NEEDLES

1 pair 3.25mm (USA 3) (UK 10)
1 pair 3.75mm (USA 5) (UK 9)
1 pair 4.00mm (USA 6) (UK 8)

BUTTONS

Version 1, left

7 x 2cm x 2.7cm oval shaped (H48 Durango)
See page 106 for Durango Button Company details.

Version 2, previous 3 pages

7 x 2cm Diameter

TENSION

22.5 sts and 30 rows measured over 10cm (approx. 4") of Stocking Stitch & Intarsia, using 4.00mm needles.

MOSS STITCH

Row 1 K1, p1 to end
Row 2 Purl all the K sts and Knit all the P sts as they face you. These two rows form pattern.

LEFT FRONT

Note; to achieve extra length for sizes C & D, the first 13 rows of the graph are knitted twice.

Using 3.75mm needles and col A, cast on 53(59,63,67)sts.

Rows 1 - 5 Col A, Moss Stitch, **Row 6** Col B, purl **Row 7** (RS) Col C, purl, **Rows 8 & 9** Col C, Moss stitch, **Row 10** Col C, purl, **Row 11** Col B, purl, **Row 12** Col A, purl, Rep rows 1 - 12, once.
Row 25 Col A, Moss stitch, **Row 26** Col A, Moss stitch, inc 6(5,6,7)sts across the row [59(64,69,74)sts].
Change to 4.00mm needles.
Now refer to graph for colour changes and working in st st, work the first 14(14,13,13) rows of patt.
Size C & D only Work rows 2 - 13 again. Work row 14. Work Row 14 again.

...continue page 34

TASHKENT GRAPH

Front, Back and Sleeves

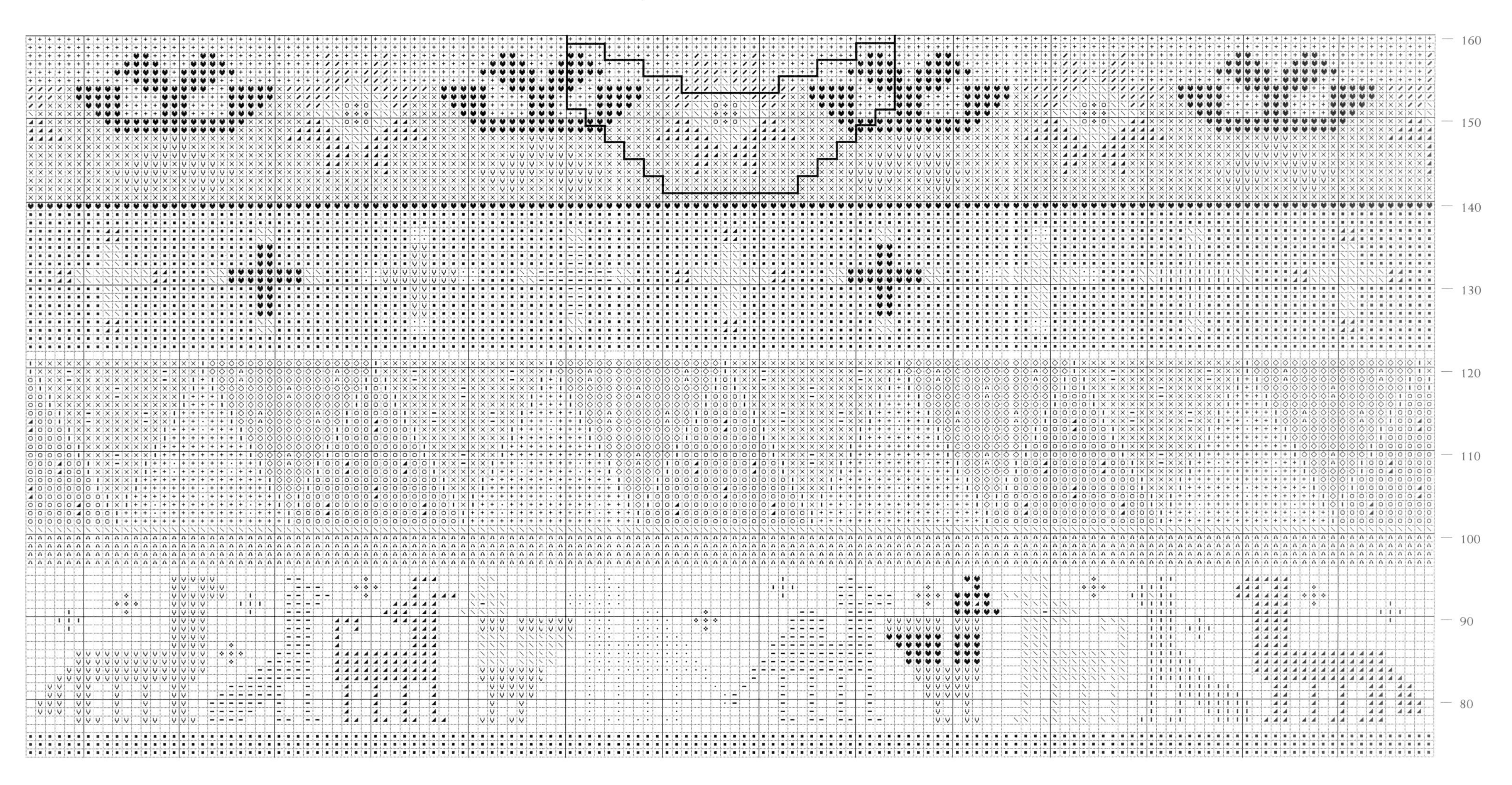

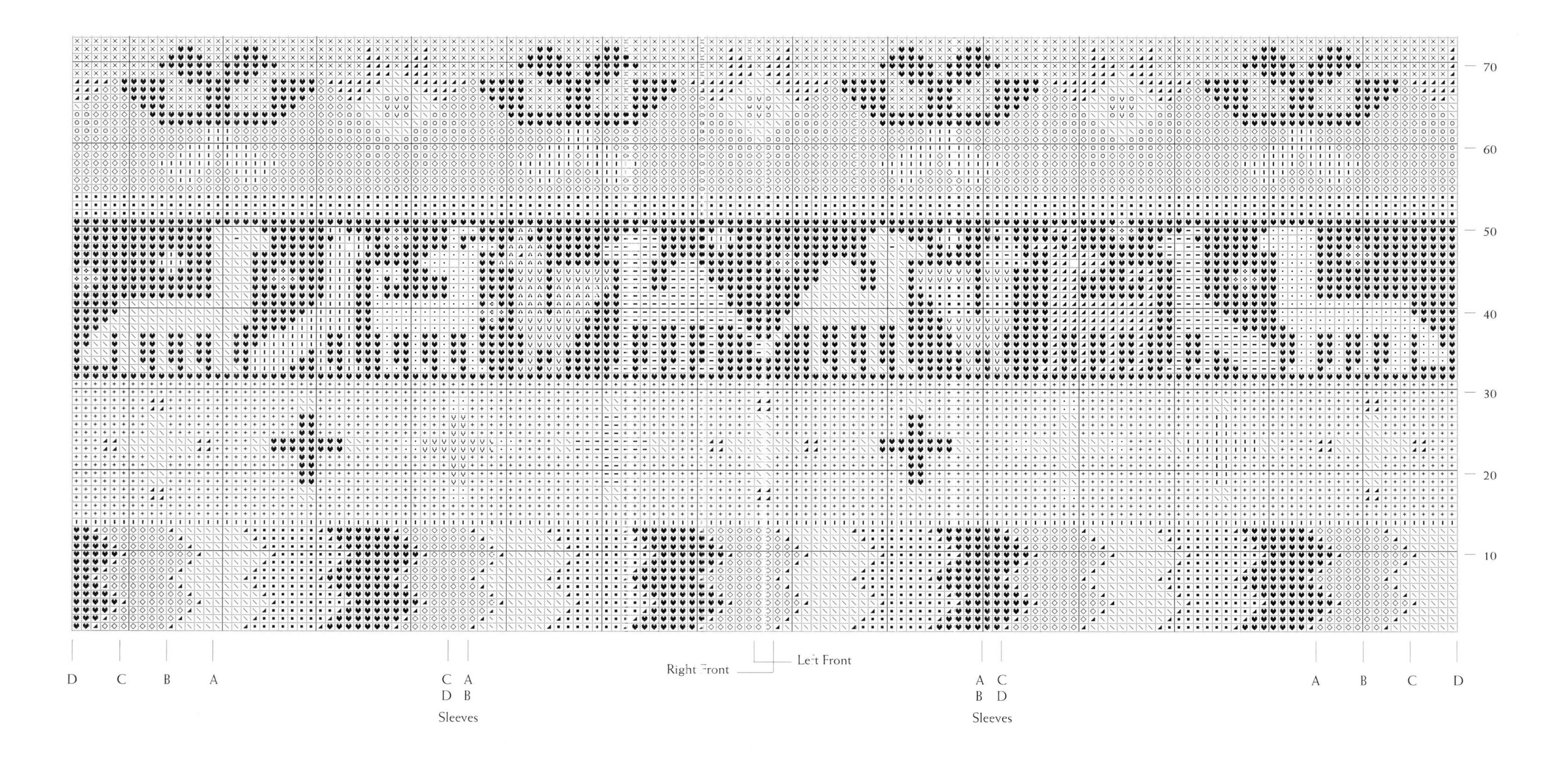
70
60
50
40
30
20
10
D
C
B
A
C A
D B
Sleeves
Right Front
Left Front
A C
B D
Sleeves
A
B
C
D

All sizes Beginning on row 15 of graph, cont to within 19(19,23,23)rows of last row [141(141,150,150)rows].
Shape neck (WS) Cast off 8(8,7,7)sts at neck edge on next row, then 2 sts at neck edge on next alt row, then 2 sts on foll alt rows 4(4,6,6)times [41(46,48,53)sts] [152(152,165,165)graph rows].
Patt 8 rows without shaping. Cast off.

RIGHT FRONT

Work right front to match left front reversing all shaping.

BACK

Using 3.75mm needles and col A, cast on 115(125,135,145)sts and work band as for front band, inc 1 st in last WS row [116(126,136,146)sts].
Change to 4.00mm needles and refer to graph for colour changes. Work in st st throughout. Work the first 14(14,13,13) rows of patt.
Size C & D only Work rows 1-13 again. Work row 14.
All sizes Beginning on row 15 of graph, cont to within 7 rows of end of graph [153(153,166,166)rows].
Shape back neck (WS) Patt 53(58,63,68)sts, cast off centre 10 sts, work to the end of row. Work each side of neck separately. Work 1 row straight. Cast off 4(4,5,5)sts at neck edge on next row, then 4(4,5,5)sts on foll alt row, twice [160(160,173,173)graph rows].
Cast off rem 41(46,48,53)sts. Work second side to match first side, reversing all shaping.

SLEEVE

Using 3.25mm needles & col A, cast on 53(53,57,57)sts.
Work 4cm Moss Stitch, inc 1 st in last WS row 54(54,58,58)sts. Change to 4.00mm needles and refer to graph for colour changes. Patt 11 rows straight.
Shape sleeve Keeping patt correct, inc 1 st at each end of every 4th row, 19(19,15,15)times, then every 3rd row 4(4,10,10)times [100(100,108,108)sts] [99(99,101,101)rows].
Work 23(23,21,21)rows without shaping (122 rows excluding band). Cast off.

MAKING UP

Press all pieces gently on WS using a warm iron over a damp cloth, taking care not to flatten Moss Stitch texture. Using Backstitch, join shoulder seams.
Centre sleeves and join, join side and sleeve seams.
Button band Using 3.25mm needles and col A, cast on 7 sts. Work in Moss st until band (when slightly stretched) is the same lengh as the front, to beg of neck shaping. Cast off. Sew band into position as you go. Mark position on band for 7 buttons, the first to come 2cm from bottom of band, the last to come 2cm from top of band, the other 5 spaced evenly between.
Buttonhole band Using 3.25mm needles and col A, cast on 7 sts and work to correspond with Button Band, keeping Moss st pattern correct and working

7 button holes opposite markers as follows; work 2 sts, cast off 3 sts, work 2 sts. On next row, cast on 3 sts in place of those cast off on previous row.
Collar With RS facing, using 4.00mm needles and col A, pick up 31(31,35,35)sts up right front neck, 35(35,41,41)sts across back neck, 31(31,35,35)sts down left front neck [97(97,111,111)sts].
Row 1 (RS) K1, p1, k1, p1, k1, k87(87,101,101), k1, p1, k1, p1, k1.
Row 2 K1, p1, k1, p1, k1, p87(87,101,101), k1, p1, k1, p1, k1.
Rep rows 1 & 2 until 18 rows (6cm) are completed.
Row 19 *K1, p1; rep from * to last k1.
Rep row 19, 7 times.
Cast off in Moss stitch. Press seams.

TASHKENT HAT

Version 1 (right) pattern given below.
Version 2 (above) use pattern below, omit colour changes.
Tension 22.5sts & 30 rows measured over 10cm Stocking stitch using 4.00mm needles.
Using 3.25mm needles and col B, cast on 116 sts and work 2cm st st ending on a WS row. Work 5 rows Garter stitch (knit all rows). Purl 1 row.
Next row (RS) K1 * yf, k2 tog; rep from * to end.
Purl 1 row.
Change to 4.00mm needles & col A and work 9cm st st.
Shape crown Change to col B and work in st st as follows;
Next row (RS) K1 [sl1, k1, psso, k15, k2tog] 6 times, k1 (104 sts).
Purl 1 row.
Next row K1, [sl1, k1, psso, k13, k2tog] 6 times, k1(92 sts).
Purl 1 row.
Cont to dec 12 sts every RS row until 20 sts remain.
Next row (RS) K2 tog across row (10sts).
Break yarn, leaving enough length for sewing.
Draw yarn through rem sts and pull tog tightly and sew seam using Backstitch.

Tashkent -Version 1, right

MEASUREMENTS

Sizes	A	(B	C	D)	
To fit bust	80	90	100	110	cm
Bodice circumference	100	110	120	130	cm
Bodice length	68	68	68	68	cm
Sleeve length	49	49	49	49	cm

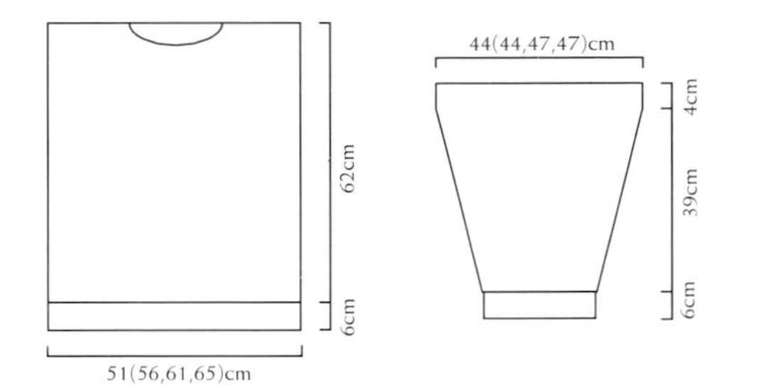

YARN

Jo Sharp 8 ply DK Pure Wool Hand Knitting Yarn

Colour	Yarn Quantity				
Sizes	A	(B	C	D)	
Version 1 (Previous 2 pages and right)					
Antique 323	19	20	21	21	x 50g balls
Version 2 (left)					
Ebony 902	21	20	20	21	x 50g balls

NEEDLES

1 pair 3.75mm needles (USA 5) (UK 9)
1 pair 4.50mm needles (USA 7) (UK 7)
1 set 3.75mm circular needles (USA 5) (UK 9)

TENSION

22.5sts and 30 rows measured over 10cm (approx 4") Stocking Stitch using 4.00mm needles.

ABBREVIATIONS

T3B **Twist 3 back,** Slip next 2 sts onto cn and hold at back of work. K next st, then P 2 sts from cn.

T3F **Twist 3 front,** Slip next st onto cn and hold at front of work. P next 2 sts, then K st from cn.

MB **Make bobble,** (k1, p1) 3 times into next st, pass 2nd, 3rd, 4th, 5th 6th sts over 1st st and off the needle.

Anastasia - Version 1, above right
Anastasia - Version 2, left

CABLE PATTERN

Row 1 *Kb1, p7, k1, Kb1, k1, p7; rep from * to end.
Row 2 And all foll alt rows, (WS) knit all k sts, purl all p sts, where MB sts occur, knit these.
Row 3 *Kb1, p5, T3B, kb1, T3F, p5; rep from * to end.
Row 5 *Kb1, p3, T3B, p2, kb1, p2, T3F, p3; rep from * to end.
Row 7 *Kb1, p1, T3B, p1, T3B, kb1, T3F, p1, T3F, p1; rep from * to end.
Row 9 *Kb1, p1, k1, p3, k1, p2, kb1, p2, k1, p3, k1, p1; rep from * to end.
Row 11 *Kb1, p1, k1, p3, MB, p2, kb1, p2, MB, p3, k1, p1, kb1, p1, k1, p6, kb1, p6, k1, p1; rep from * to end.
Row 13 *Kb1, p1, MB, p6, kb1, p6, MB, p1, kb1, p8, kb1, p8; rep from * to end.
Row 14 As row 2.
These 14 rows form patt rep.

FRONT

Using 3.75mm needles, cast on 135(145,160,170)sts, and work in rib as follows;

Row 1 *K1, p1, k1, p2; rep from * to end.

Row 2 *K2, p1, k1, p1; rep from * to end.

Rep these two rows until rib measures 6cm, inc 0(0,3,1)sts in last WS row [135(145,163,171)sts].

Change to 4.50mm needles.

Next Row Work 4(9,0,4)sts in rev st st, then work Row 1 of Cable Pattern, rep to last 5(10,1,5)sts, Kb1, work to the end in rev st st .

This row sets position of pattern.

Cont on patt until work measures 61(61,61,61)cm, including band and ending on a WS row **.

Shape neck Patt 55(60,69,73)sts, turn and leave rem 80(85,94,98)sts on a holder.

Work each side of neck separately.

Cast off 2 sts at neck edge on next row, and foll alt rows twice, then 1 st on foll alt rows, 3 times 46(51,60,64)sts.

Work 10 rows without shaping, cast off.

With RS facing, leave 25 sts on holder, rejoin yarn to rem sts and complete second side to match first side, reversing all shaping.

BACK

Work as for front to**. Cont without shaping until back bodice length matches front bodice length.

Cast off.

SLEEVES

Using 3.75mm needles, cast on 55(55,65,65)sts and work 6cm in rib as for Front, increasing 10(10,8,8) sts evenly across last WS row [65(65,73,73)sts].

Change to 4.50mm needles.

Row 1 Work 5(5,9,9)sts in rev st st, 55 sts from Row 1 of Cable Pattern, then work 5(5,9,9)sts in rev st st.

This row sets patt. Cont on patt at set, AT THE SAME TIME shape sleeve by inc 1 st at each end (in Reverse st st) of every 4th row, 20 times then every 3rd row, 10 times [125(125,133,133)sts] (110 rows).

Work 15 rows straight, adjust length here if desired.

Cast off evenly.

MAKING UP

Press all pieces gently on WS using a warm iron over a damp cloth. Using Backstitch, join shoulder seams. Centre sleeves and join. Join side and sleeve seams using Edge to Edge stitch on ribs.

Collar With RS facing, using a 3.75mm circular needle, pick up and knit 28 sts down left front neck, 25 sts from holder at front, 28 sts up right front neck and 51 sts across back neck (132 sts). Work in rounds of k2, p2 rib for 15 cm. Cast off evenly in rib.

Anastasia - Version 2, right

MIRAGE

MIRAGE

MEASUREMENTS

Unisex sizes	A	(B	C	D)	
To fit chest/bust	80-90	90-100	100-110	110-120	cm
Bodice Circumference	110	120	130	140	cm
Bodice Length	64	66	74	74	cm
Sleeve length	39	39	43	43	cm

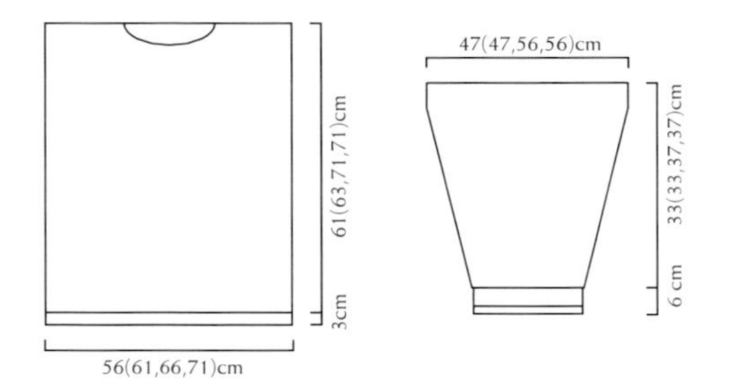

YARN

Jo Sharp 8ply DK Pure Wool Handknitting Yarn

Colour	Yarn Quanitiy				
Unisex Sizes	A	(B	C	D)	
Sweater Version 1 (worn by man)					
Antique 323	16	16	18	20	x 50 g balls
Sweater Version 2 (worn by woman)					
Storm 706	16	16	18	20	x 50 g balls

NEEDLES

1 pair 3.25mm needles (USA 3) (UK 10)
1 pair 3.75mm needles (USA 5) (UK 9)
1 pair 4.00mm needles (USA 6) (UK 8)
1 Cable needle

TENSION

22.5sts and 30 rows measured over 10cm (approx. 4") Stocking Stitch using 4.00mm needles.

FRONT

Using 3.25mm needles, cast on 106(116,126,136)sts and work 12 rows Garter stitch (knit all rows) inc 22 sts evenly across the last row 128(138,148,158)sts.
Change to 4.00mm needles, and refer to Bodice Graph Part 1 and work 20 rows in patt as indicated.
Work 58(64,96,96)rows st st [30(32,43,43)cm incl. band].
Now refer to Bodice Graph Part 1 and beg on a RS work rows 1 - 18.

Next Row (RS) Knit, inc 22(24,26,28)sts evenly across row [150(162,174,186)sts].
Next Row Knit.
Now refer to Bodice Graph Part 2 and beg on a RS row work first 2 rows of graph.
Cont on 12 row repeat until work (incl. band) measures 55(57,65,65)cm, ending on a WS row.
Shape neck Work 68(74,80,86)sts, turn and leave rem 82(88,94,100)sts on a holder. Work each side of neck separately. Cast off 2 sts at neck edge on next row, then 2 sts on every alt row 2(2,6,6)times, then 1 st on alt rows 7(7,3,3)times [55(61,63,69)sts] (20 rows of neck shaping). Work 8 rows without shaping. Cast off.
Rejoin yarn to rem sts and cast off 14 centre sts. Work second side to match first side, reversing all shaping.

BACK

Work back bodice to match front bodice, omitting front neck shaping and working back neck shaping into last 6 rows as follows;
(RS) Work 68(74,80,86)sts, turn and leave rem 82(88,94,100)sts on a holder. Cast off 6(6,8,8)sts at neck edge on next row, then 4(4,5,5)sts on foll alt row, then 3(3,4,4)sts on foll alt row. Cast off rem 55(61,63,69)sts. Rejoin yarn to rem sts and cast off 14 centre sts, then work second side to match first side, reversing all shaping.

SLEEVE

Note; It is advised when knitting this unisex garment for a Man (any size) to use the size D sleeve.
Sleeve is worked from top and finishing at cuff.
Using 4.00 mm needles, cast on 106(106,126,126)sts.
Work 1 row st st. Now refer to graph (4 row pattern repeat) and work 4(4,3,3)rows without shaping [5(5,4,4)rows].
Shape sleeve Keeping 4 row pattern repeat correct, dec 1 st at each end of next row, then 1 st at each end of foll 4th(4th,3rd,3rd)rows, 10(10,16,16)times, then on foll 5th rows, 1(1,0,0)times, [82(82,92,92)sts] [51(51,53,53)rows] [16(16,17,17)cm].

Sleeve Graph

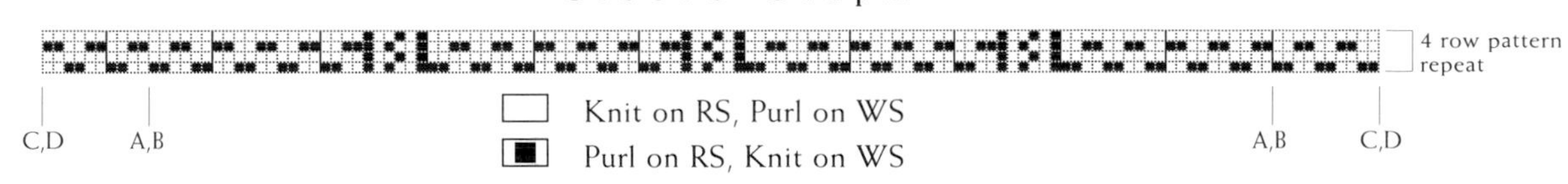

Mirage - Version 1, left , Version 2, far left
Mirage - Version 2, previous 2 pages

Make Ridge

Row 52(52,54,54) (WS) Knit.
Row 53(53,55,55) Knit.
Row 54(54,56,56) Purl.
Row 55(55,57,57) Purl.
Row 56(56,58,58) Purl.

Now cont in st st, shaping as you go.

Dec 1 st at each end of every 3rd(3rd,4th,4th)row, 10(10,13,13)times, then every 6th(6th,0,0)row, 2(2,0,0)times. Work 1 row. Adjust length here if desired [58(58,66,66)sts] [99(99,111,111)rows] [33(33,37,37)cm from beg].

Make Ridge

Row 100(100,112,112) (WS)Knit.
Row 101(101,113,113) Knit.
Row 102(102,114,114) Purl.
Row 103(103,115,115) Purl.
Row 104(104,116,116) Purl.

Cuff Texture

Row 105(105,117,117) (RS) *K2, p2; rep from * to end.
Row 106(106,118,118) Purl
Row 107(107,119,119) *P2, k2; rep from * to end.
Row 108(108,120,120) Purl.

Rep the last 4 rows, 3 times [120(120,132,132)rows]. (16 rows of Texture in all).

Next Row (RS) Purl.

Now work in st st for 8 rows, dec 5 sts evenly across last row. Cast off loosely and evenly.

MAKING UP

Press all pieces gently with a warm iron over a damp cloth. Join right shoulder seam.

Neckband *Note; Two versions are given, either version is suitable for men or women's sweater.*

Version 1 (shown on man)

With RS facing, using 3.75mm needles, pick up and knit 64(64,72,72)st evenly around front neck, and 40(40,48,48)sts across back neck [104(104,120,120)sts]. work in K1, p1 rib until neckband measures 7cm.

Version 2 (shown on woman)

Pick up sts as for Version 1 and working in rows as follows;

Row 1 WS *P1, k1, p2, k1, p1, k1, p1; rep from * to end.
Row 2 *K1, p1; rep from * to end.

Rep rows 1 and 2 until neckband measures 7cm.
Join collar seam and left shoulder.
Centre sleeves and join, join side and sleeve seams.
Press seams.

KEY

☐ K on RS, P on WS
■ P on RS, K on WS

C4F **Cable 4 Front,** slip next 2 sts onto cable needle and hold at front of work, knit next 2 sts from left-hand needle, then knit sts from cable needle.

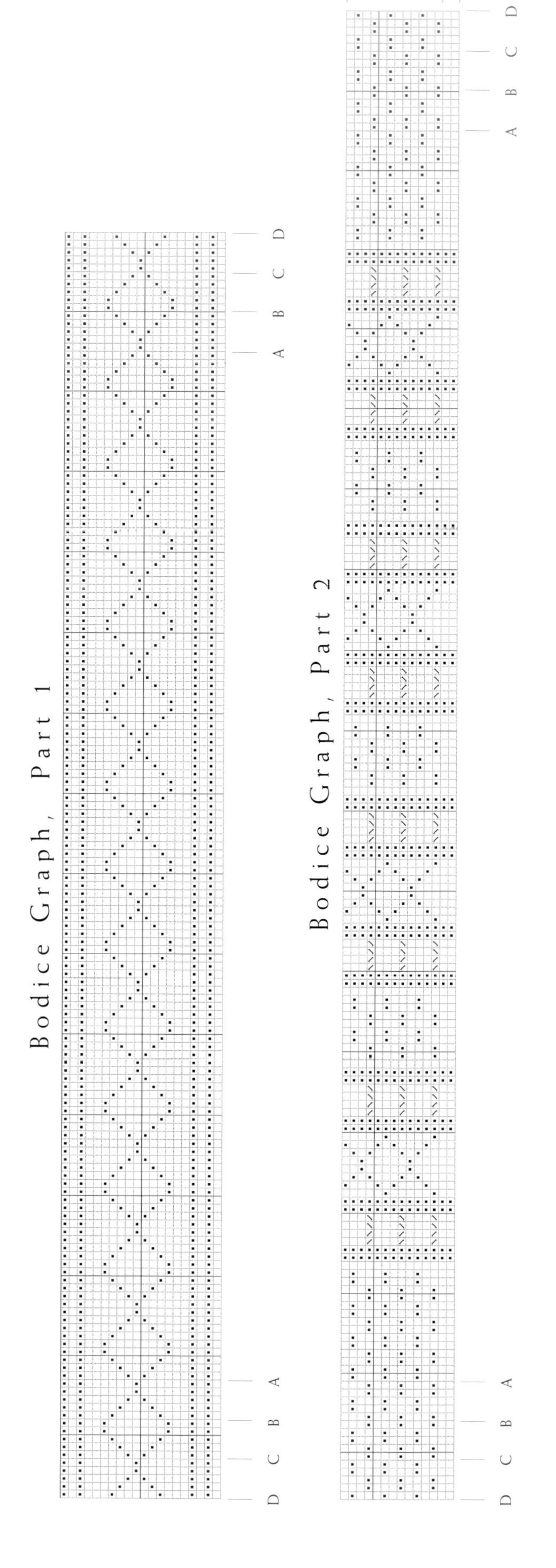

Sweater - Version 1, right

BALTHAZAR

MEASUREMENTS

Hat; One size fits all.

Sweaters

Unisex sizes	A	(B	C	D)	
To fit chest/bust	80-90	90-100	100-110	110-120	cm
Bodice circumference	114	128	138	144	cm
Bodice length	66	66	70	70	cm
Sleeve length	46	46	51	51	cm

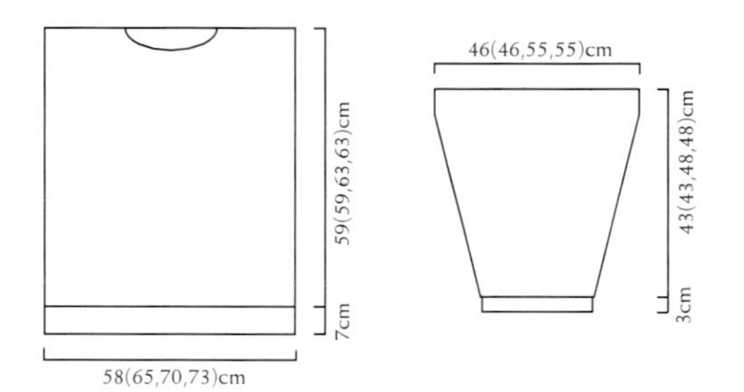

YARN

Jo Sharp 8 ply DK Pure Wool Hand Knitting Yarn

Code	Key	Colour	Yarn Quantity				
Unisex Sizes			A	(B	C	D)	
Women's Sweater (left)							
A	☐	Wine 307	15	15	16	16	x 50g balls
B	■	Tangerine 003	5	5	5	5	x 50g balls
	+	Heron 802	1	1	1	1	x 50g ball
Men's Sweater (next page)							
A	☐	Slate 328	16	17	17	18	x 50g balls
B	■	Ginger 322	5	5	5	5	x 50g balls
	+	Antique 323	1	1	1	1	x 50g ball

Hat (left)

One size fits all.

A	☐	Tangerine 003	1	x 50g ball
B	■	Heron 802	1	x 50g ball
C	+	Wine 307	1	x 50g ball

NEEDLES

1 pair 4.00mm needles (USA 6) (UK 8)
3.75mm circular needle (USA 5) (UK 9)
1 pair 4.50mm needles (USA 7) (UK 7)
Hat only; 3.25mm needles (USA 3) (UK 10)

TENSION

Stocking Stitch; 22.5 sts and 30 rows measured over 10cm (approx. 4") using 4.00mm needles
Fairisle; 25 sts and 25 rows measured over 10cm (approx 4") using 4.50mm needles.

Balthazar - Women's Sweater, left

FRONT

Using 4.00mm needles and col A, cast on 146(162,174,182)sts, then joining in col B, work in k2, p2 two colour rib, stranding yarn at back of work as for Fairisle as follows;

Row 1 (RS) *K2, col B, p2, col A; rep from * to last 2 sts, k2, col B.

Row 2 (WS) P2 col B * k2 col A, p2, col B; rep from * to end.

Repeat these two rows 9 times (20 rows in all)

Change to 4.50mm needles, refer to graph for fairisle pattern and work 96 rows (38 cm excluding band).

Row 97 (RS) Keeping patt correct, dec 20sts evenly across last row of pattern [126(142,154,162)sts].

Change to 4.00mm needles and cont in st st using col A until work measures 51(51,55,55)cm, excluding band and ending on a WS row. Adjust length here if desired.

Shape neck Work 51(59,65,69)sts, turn and leave rem 75(83,89,93)sts on a holder. Work each side of neck separately. Cast off 2 sts at beg of next row, then 2 sts at neck edge on foll alt row, then 1 st on every alt row, 4 times. Work 12 rows without shaping. Cast off. With RS facing, rejoin yarn to rem sts and cast off 24 sts from holder, then complete second side to match first side, rev all shaping.

BACK

Work to match Front bodice length, excluding neck shaping.

SLEEVES

It is advised, when knitting this unisex garment in size A, B, C or D for a man, to use the C or D sleeve.

Using 4.00mm needles & col A, cast on 54(54,64,64)sts and work 8 rows st st. Work 4 rows k2, p2 rib.

Work 1 row st st. Cont in st st AT THE SAME TIME shape sides as follows; Inc 1 st at each end of every 4th row, 15(15,30,30)times. Work 1 row.

Now inc 1 st at each end of every 5th(5th,0,0)row, 10(10,0,0)times [104(104,124,124)sts] [112(112,122,122)rows]. Work 17(17,21,21)rows without shaping (adjust length here if desired).

Cast off.

COLLAR

Using 3.75mm circular needles and col A, cast on 128 sts, knit 9 rounds.

Shape collar

Round 10 K126, sl1, k1, psso.

Round 11 K2tog, k48, sl1, k1, psso, k2tog, k73.
Round 12 & 13 Knit.
Round 14 K122, sl1, k1, psso.
Round 15 K2tog, k46, sl1, k1, psso, k2tog, k71.
Round 16 & 17 Knit.
Round 18 K118, sl1, k1, psso.
Round 19 K2tog, k44, sl1, k1, psso, k2tog, k69.
Round 20 & 21 Knit.
Round 22 K114, sl1, k1, psso.
Round 23 K2tog, k42, sl1, k1, psso, k2tog, k67.
Round 24 & 25 Knit.
Round 26 K110, sl1, k1, psso.
Round 27 K2tog, k40, sl1, k1, psso, k2tog, k65.
Round 28 & 29 Knit.
Round 30 K106, k1, sl1, psso.
Round 31 K2tog, k38, sl1, k1, psso, k2tog, k63.
Cont working in rounds until collar measures 20cm.

MAKING UP

Press all pieces (except ribbing) on WS with a warm iron over a damp cloth. Using Backstitch, join shoulder seams. Centre sleeves and join, join side and sleeve seams, using Edge to Edge stitch on ribs and reversing seam at cuff.

Sew in collar Using Edge to Edge stitch, join collar seam. Position collar into neck hole and join, leaving 1cm st st curling towards outside of garment (as in illustration) Press seams.

BALTHAZAR HAT

Using 3.25mm needles and col A, cast on 116 sts and work 2cm st st ending on a WS row. Now work 2cm k2, p2 rib, ending on a WS row. Change to 4.00mm needles and work 4 rows Garter (knit all rows). Cont in st st for 6cm, ending on a WS row. Work 4 rows Garter st. Change to col B and work 2 rows st st. Change to col A and work 4 rows Garter st.

Shape crown (RS) K1 [sl1, k1, psso, k15, k2tog] 6 times, k1 (104 sts).

Purl 1 row.

Next row K1, [sl1, k1, psso, k13, k2tog]6 times, k1 (92 sts).

Purl 1 row.

Cont working in st st, dec 12 sts every RS row until 20 sts remain.

Next row (RS) K2 tog across row (10sts).

Break yarn, leaving enough length for sewing

Draw yarn through rem sts and pull tog tightly and sew seam using Backstitch.

Embroider motifs to hat Using Swiss Darning or Duplicate Stitch technique, and col B, work 7 star motifs (see Hat graph above right) with 9 stitch intervals. Work centre stitch of each motif in col C. Place a second row of star motifs as illustrated.

Balthazar - hat

Hat Graph

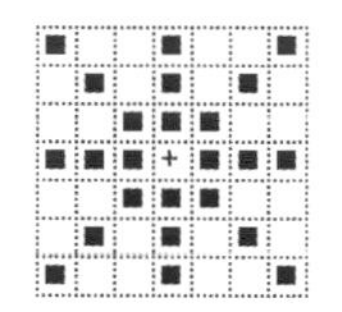

Bodice Front & Back Graph

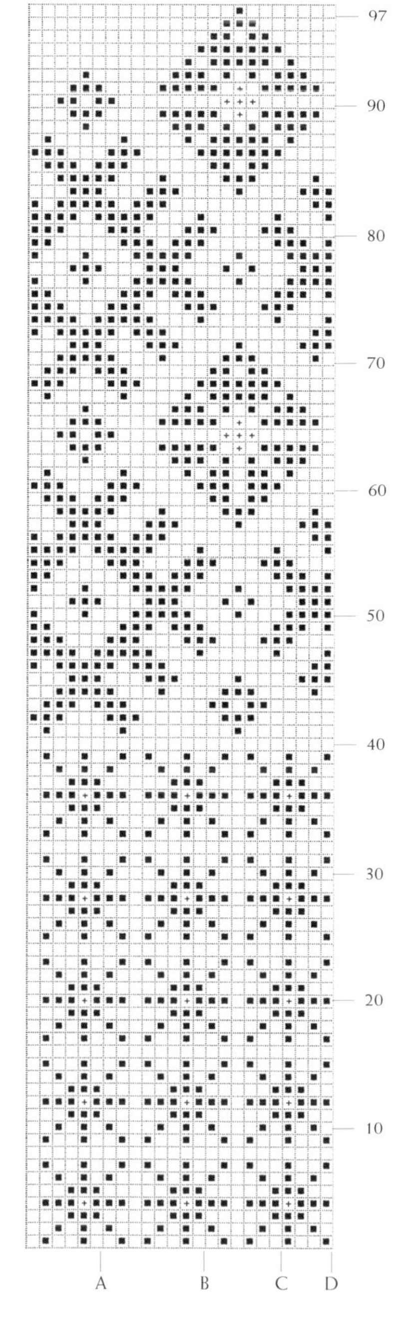

Graph note; Begin working at position marked for size being knitted and work left. Then work from far right to left in repeat for remainder of row.
This row sets position for pattern.

Balthazar - Men's Sweater, right

ARABELLA

MEASUREMENTS

Sizes	A	(B	C	D)	
To fit bust	80	90	100	110	cm
Bodice circumference	86	96	106	116	cm
Bodice length	59	59	61	61	cm
Sleeve seam 3/4 length	27	27	25	25	cm
Sleeve seam full length	42	42	41	41	cm

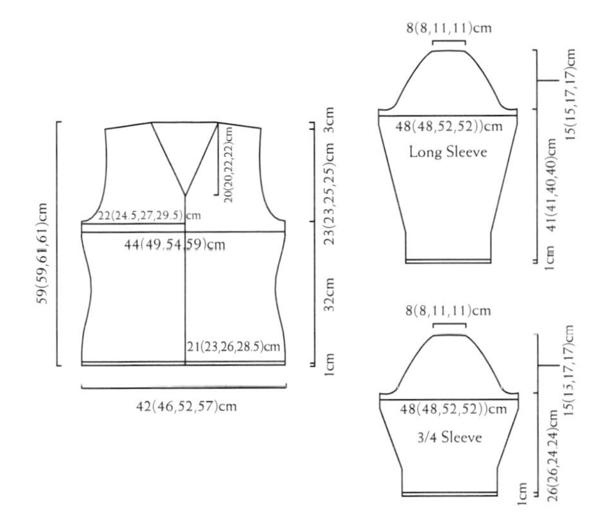

YARN

Jo Sharp 8 ply DK Pure Wool Hand Knitting Yarn

Colour	Yarn Quantity				
Sizes	A	(B	C	D)	
Grey cardigan (left)					
Owl 801	11	12	13	14	x 50g balls
Red cardigan (previous 2 pages)					
Cherry 309	11	12	13	14	x 50g balls
Black cardigan 3/4 sleeve (next page)					
Black 302	10	11	12	13	x 50g balls

NEEDLES

1 pair 3.25mm needles (USA 3) (UK 10)
1 pair 4.00mm needles (USA 6) (UK 8)

BUTTONS

6 x 12mm buttons

Arabella - Grey Cardigan, left
Arabella - Red Cardigan, previous 2 pages

TENSION

22.5 sts and 30 rows measured over 10cm (approx. 4") of Stocking Stitch using 4.00mm needles.

BACK

Using 3.25mm needles, cast on 94(104,116,128)sts.
Row 1 Knit
Row 2 (RS) Purl
Change to 4.00mm needles
Row 3 Purl
Row 4 (RS) Knit
Work 26 rows st st (beg purl row) (30 rows including band). Cont in st st throughout.
Shape bodice (RS) Dec 1 st at each end of next row, then foll alt row, once, then every 4th row, 5 times. [80(90,102,114)sts] (53 rows).
Work 7 rows straight, then inc 1 st at each end of next row, then foll alt rows, 3 times, then every 3rd row, 6 times [100(110,122,134)sts] (85 rows).
Work 11 rows without shaping (96 rows incl. band).
Shape armholes (RS) Cast off 6(6,8,8)sts at beg next 2 rows, then dec 1 st at each end of every row, 5(5,8,8) times, then every alt row, 4(4,3,3)times [70(80,84,96)sts] [111(111,112,112)rows].
Work 55(55,60,60)rows without shaping [166(166,172,172)rows, incl. band].
Shape shoulders Cast off 4(6,6,7)sts at beg on next 4 rows, then 5(6,6,7)sts at beg of next 2 rows.
Cast off rem 44(44,48,54)sts.

LEFT FRONT

Using 3.25mm needles, cast on 47(52,58,64)sts.
Work rows 1 - 4 as per Back. Work 26 rows st st (30 rows). Cont in st st throughout.
Shape bodice (RS) Dec 1 st at (beg) seam edge of next row, then foll alt row, once, then every 4th row, 5 times. [40(45,51,57)sts] (53 rows).
Work 7 rows straight, then inc 1 st at seam edge of next row, then foll alt rows, 3 times, then every 3rd row, 6 times [50(55,61,67)sts] (85 rows). Work 11 rows without shaping (96 rows, including band).
Shape armhole Cast off 6(6,8,8)sts at beg of next row, work 1 row, then dec 1 st at armhole edge in every row 5(5,8,8)times, then every alt row 4(4,3,3)times. Work 1(1,0,0)rows without shaping. [35(40,42,48)sts] (112 rows). Cont working armhole edge straight, AT THE SAME TIME,

Shape neck (RS) Dec 1 st at neck edge on next row, then foll 3rd row, 15(15,18,18)times [19(24,23,29)sts] [158(158,167,167)rows].
Work 8(8,5,5)rows without shaping [166(166,172,172)rows, including band].
Shape shoulder (RS) Cast off 4(6,6,7)sts at beg of next row, then foll alt row once, then 5(6,6,7)sts on next alt row. Work 1 row, cast off rem 6(6,5,8)sts.

RIGHT FRONT

Make Right Front to match Left Front, reversing all shaping.

SLEEVES

(3/4 length version)

Using 3.25mm needles, cast on 46(46,52,52)sts.
Work rows 1 - 4 as per Back.
Work 4 rows st st (8 rows). Cont in st st.*
Shape sleeve Inc 1 st at each end of every 3rd row, 10(10,2,2)times, then every alt row, 21(21,30,30)times [108(108,116,116)sts] [80(80,74,74)rows, including band].
Shape sleeve cap Cast off 6(6,8,8)sts at beg of next 2 rows, then dec 1 st at each end of every foll row, 6 times, then every alt row 9(9,13,13)times, then 1 st at each end of every row 6(6,10,10)times. Cast off 3 sts at beg of next 12(12,6,6)rows. Cast off rem 18(18,24,24)sts, [44(44,50,50) rows of sleeve cap shaping].

SLEEVES

(Full length version)

Work as for 3/4 length version to *
Shape sleeve Inc 1 st at each end of every 4th row, 25 times, then every 3rd(3rd,2nd,2nd)row, 6(6,7,7)times [108(108,116,116)sts] [126(126,122,122)rows, including band]
Work Sleeve Cap as for 3/4 length version.

MAKING UP

Press all pieces, gently on WS using a warm iron over a damp cloth. Using Backstitch, join shoulder seams, Centre sleeves and join. Join side and sleeve seams.
Button band With RS facing, using 3.25mm needles, pick up and K 16(16,19,19)sts across half back neck to beg neck shaping on left side, 57(57,62,62)sts down left side neck shaping, 96 sts down left side to bottom edge. [169(169,177,177)sts].
Row 1 Purl.
Row 2 (RS)Knit.
Row 3 Knit.
Row 4 Purl.
Cast off knitwise.
Mark positions for 6 buttons, the first to come 1cm from bottom edge on left side, the last to be positioned at beginning of neck shaping, the remaining 4 to be spaced evenly between.
Buttonhole band With RS facing, using 3.25mm needles, pick up and knit 96sts up right side to beginning of neck shaping, 57(57,62,62)sts along neck shaping and 16(16,19,19)sts across half back neck [169(169,177,177) sts].
Row 1 (Button hole row) (WS) Purl this row, making six, 2 stitch button holes to correspond with markers.
Row 2 Knit, casting on sts where sts were previously cast off for button holes.
Row 3 Knit
Row 4 Purl.
Cast off knitwise. Sew buttons in place. Press seams.

Arabella - Black Cardigan with 3/4 sleeve, left

MILLEFIORI

MILLEFIORI

MEASUREMENTS

Sizes	A	(B	C	D)	
To fit bust	80	90	100	110	cm
Bodice circumference	86	96	106	116	cm
Bodice length	53	53	55	55	cm
Sleeve seam length	42	42	42	42	cm

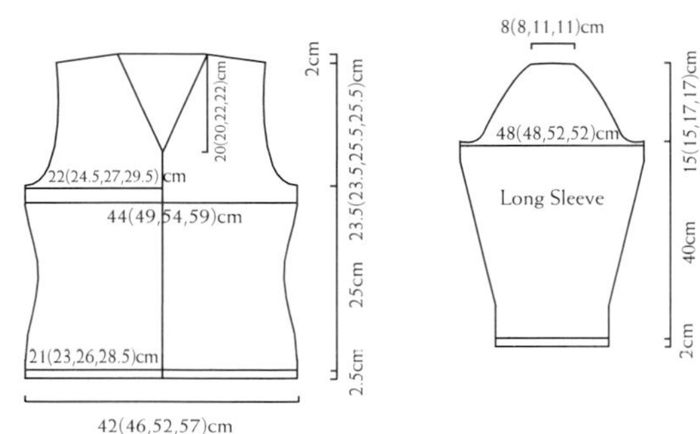

YARN

Jo Sharp 8 ply DK Pure Wool Hand Knitting Yarn

Code	Key	Colour	A	(B	C	D)	
			Yarn Quantity				
Version 1 (left)							
A	☐	Mosaic 336	9	9	9	10	x 50g balls
	+	Ink 901	1	1	1	1	x 50g ball
	☒	Orchard 906	1	1	1	1	x 50g ball
	I	Miro 507	1	1	1	1	x 50g ball
	▪	Navy 327	1	1	1	1	x 50g ball
	■	Jade 316	1	1	1	1	x 50g ball
	∩	Forest 318	1	1	1	1	x 50g ball
	♥	Aegean 504	1	1	1	1	x 50g ball
Version 2 (previous 2 pages)							
A	☐	Navy 327	9	9	9	10	x 50g balls
	+	Violet 319	1	1	1	1	x 50g ball
	☒	Ginger 322	1	1	1	1	x 50g ball
	I	Owl 801	1	1	1	1	x 50g ball
	▪	Mulberry 325	1	1	1	1	x 50g ball
	■	Jade 316	1	1	1	1	x 50g ball
	∩	Forest 318	1	1	1	1	x 50g ball
	♥	Ruby 326	1	1	1	1	x 50g ball

NEEDLES

1 pair 3.25mm needles (USA 3) (UK 10)
1 pair 4.00mm needles (USA 6) (UK 8)

BUTTONS

6 x 12mm buttons

Millefiori - Version 1, left
Millefiori - Version 2, previous 2 pages

TENSION

22.5 sts & 30 rows measured over 10cm (approx. 4") of Stocking Stitch and Intarsia, using 4.00mm needles.

MOSS STITCH

Row 1 *K1, p1, rep; from * to last K1.
Row 2 As row 1.

BACK

Using 3.25mm needles and col A, cast on 93(103,115,127)sts and work 10 rows Moss Stitch, increasing 1 st in last (WS)row [94(104,116,128)sts]. Change to 4.00mm needles. Refer to Bodice Graph (50 row pattern repeat) for colour changes and cont in st st throughout. Work 10 rows.

Shape bodice (RS) Dec 1 st at each end of next row, then foll alt row, once, then every 4th row, 5 times. [80(90,102,114)sts].

Work 7 rows straight, then inc 1 st at each end of next row, then foll alt rows, 3 times, then every 3rd row, 6 times [100(110,122,134)sts] (55 rows of shaping). Work 11 rows without shaping (approx. 25cm excluding band).

Shape armholes (RS) Cast off 6(6,8,8)sts at beg next 2 rows, then dec 1 st at each end of every row, 5(5,8,8) times, then every alt row, 4(4,3,3)times [70(80,84,96)sts]. Work 55(55,60,60)rows without shaping [146(146,152,152)rows, 49(49,51,51)cm excluding band].

Shape shoulders Cast off 4(6,6,7)sts at beg on next 4 rows, then 5(6,6,7)sts at beg of next 2 rows.
Cast off rem 44(44,48,54)sts.

LEFT FRONT

Using 3.25mm needles and col A, cast on 47(51,57,63)sts. Work 10 rows Moss Stitch, increasing 0(1,1,1)st in last (WS) row [47(52,58,64)sts].

Change to 4.00mm needles. Refer to Bodice Graph (50 row pattern repeat) for colour changes and cont in st st throughout. Work 10 rows.

Shape bodice (RS) Dec 1 st at (beg) seam edge of next row, then foll alt row, once, then every 4th row, 5 times. [40(45,51,57)sts]. Work 7 rows straight, then inc 1 st at seam edge of next row, then foll alt rows, 3 times, then every 3rd row, 6 times [50(55,61,67)sts] (55 rows of shaping). Work 11 rows without shaping (approx. 25cm excluding band).

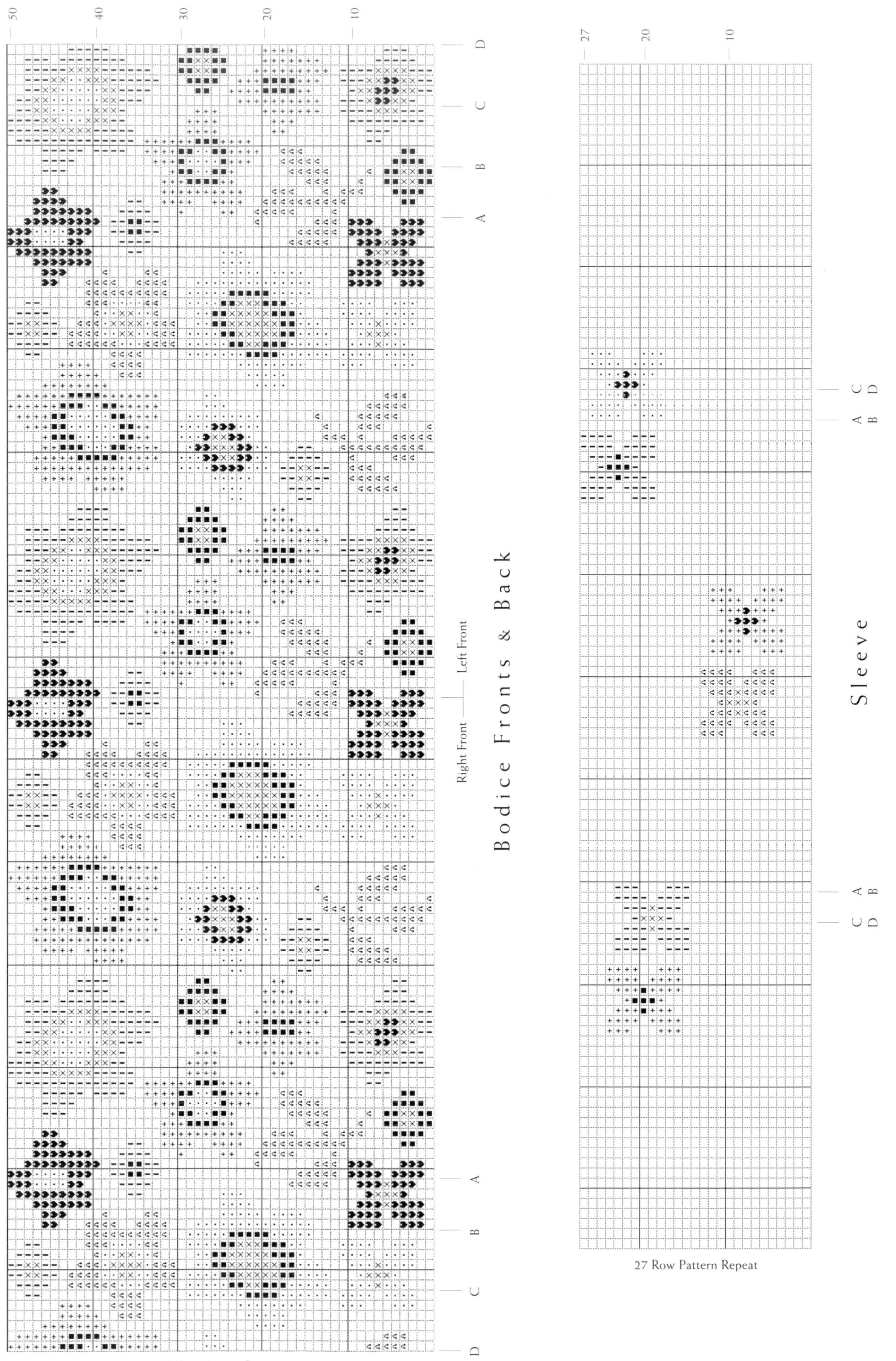
50
40
30
20
10
D
C
B
A
Right Front
Left Front
Bodice Fronts & Back
A
B
C
D
50 Row Pattern Repeat
27
20
10
C
D
A
B
Sleeve
A
B
C
D
27 Row Pattern Repeat

Shape armhole Cast off 6(6,8,8)sts at beg of next row, work 1 row, then dec 1 st at armhole edge in every row 5(5,8,8)times, then every alt row 4(4,3,3)times. [35(40,42,48)sts]. Cont working armhole edge straight; AT THE SAME TIME.

Shape neck (RS) Dec 1 st at neck edge on next row, then foll 3rd row, 15(15,18,18)times [19(24,23,29)sts]. Work 9(9,5,5)rows without shaping [146(146,152,152)rows, 49(49,51,51)cm, excluding band].

Shape shoulder (RS) Cast off 4(6,6,7)sts at beg of next row, then foll alt row once, then 5(6,6,7)sts on next alt row.

Work 1 row, cast off rem 6(6,5,8)sts.

RIGHT FRONT

Refer to graph for Right Front positioning and make Right Front to match Left Front, reversing all shaping.

SLEEVES

Using 3.25mm needles and col A, cast on 43(43,49,49)sts and work 8 rows Moss Stitch, increasing 3 sts in last (WS) row [46(46,52,52)sts]. Change to 4.00mm needles. Refer to Sleeve Graph (27 row pattern repeat) for colour changes and work in st st throughout.

Shape sleeve Inc 1 st at each end of every 4th row, 25 times, then every 3rd row, 6(6,7,7)times [108(108,116,116)sts, 118(118,121,121)rows excluding band]. Work 3(3,0,0)rows straight (121 rows).

Shape sleeve cap Cast off 6(6,8,8)sts at beg of next 2 rows, then dec 1 st at each end of every foll row, 6 times, then every alt row 9(9,13,13)times, then 1 st at each end of every row 6(6,10,10)times. Cast off 3 sts at beg of next 12(12,6,6)rows. Cast off rem 18(18,24,24)sts, [44(44,50,50) rows of sleeve cap shaping].

MAKING UP

Press all pieces, gently on WS using a warm iron over a damp cloth. Using Backstitch, join shoulder seams, centre sleeves and join. Join side and sleeve seams.

Button band Using 3.25mm needles and col A, cast on 7 sts and work in Moss stitch until band (when slightly stretched) is the same length as left front to beg of neck shaping, ending on a WS row.

Shape top band Cont in Moss st, inc 1 st at beg of next (RS) row, then inc 1 st at beg of every foll 4th row, 13(13,14,14)times [21(21,22,22)sts] [53(53,57,57)rows of shaping]. Work 1 row, cast off. Sew left side band in place. Place markers for buttons, the first to come 1cm from bottom edge, the last to be positioned at beginning of neck shaping, the remaining 4 to be spaced evenly between.

Button hole band Make Button hole band to match button band, reversing all shaping and working button holes to correspond with button markers. Sew buttons to button band.

Collar Using 3.25mm needles and col A, cast on 71(71,75,75)sts and work 1 row Moss Stitch. Cont in Moss, inc 1 st at each end of next row, then every alt row, 4(4,5,5)times.

[81(81,87,87)sts] [10(10,12,12)rows].

Work 15(15,19,19)rows without shaping. Cast off. Using Edge to Edge stitch, centre cast on edge of collar on back neck and sew into position around neckline. Join sides of collar to top of lapels, along angled edge, leaving 4.5cm straight edge of collar unsewn. See illustration for finished look of collar. Press seams.

Millefiori - Version 1, above

STELLAR

MEASUREMENTS

Sizes	A	(B	C	D)	
To fit bust	80	90	100	110	cm
Bodice circumference	108	118	126	136	cm
Bodice length (cropped)	53	53	56	56	cm
Bodice length (long)	71	71	74	74	cm
Sleeve seam length	44	44	44	44	cm

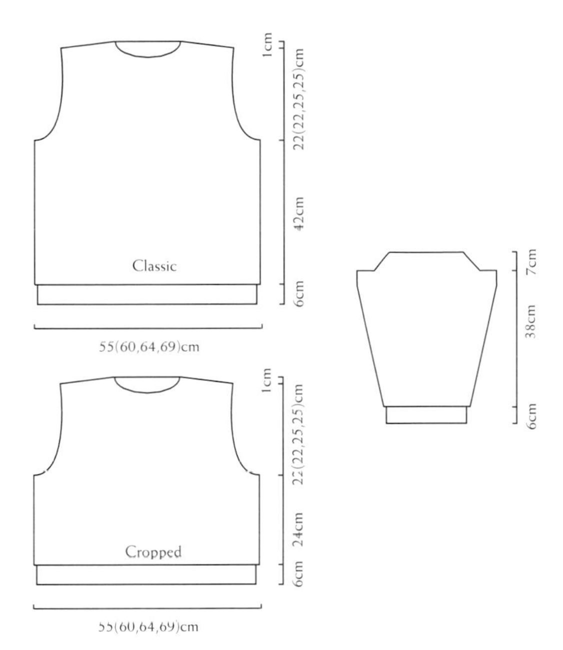

YARN

Jo Sharp 8 ply DK Pure Wool Hand Knitting Yarn

Colour	Yarn Quantity				
Sizes	A	(B	C	D)	
Cropped Sweater (left)					
Pistachio 002	12	12	13	13	x 50g balls
Long Sweater (previous 2 pages)					
Silk 903	15	15	15	16	x 50g balls

NEEDLES

1 pair 3.25mm needles (USA 3) (UK 10)
1 pair 4.00mm needles (USA 6) (UK 8)
1 set 3.75mm circular needles (USA 5) (UK 9)

TENSION

22.5 sts and 30 rows measured over 10cm (approx 4") of Stocking Stitch, using 4.00mm needles.

FRONT

Using 4.00mm needles, cast on 124(134,144,154)sts.
Row 1 (RS)*K4, p1; rep from * to last k4.
Row 2 *P4, k1; rep from * to last p4.
Repeat rows 1 & 2 until work measures 6cm, increasing 1 st in last WS row [125(135,145,155)sts].
Work 4 rows rev st st. Now refer to Bodice graph (58 row pattern repeat) and work in texture pattern until work, including band, measures (30 cm, cropped version) or (48 cm, long version) ending on a WS row.
Shape armhole Cast off 7 sts at beg of next 2 rows, then dec 1 st at beg of every foll row, 20 times [91(101,111,121)sts].
Cont in patt until work, including band, measures [49(49,52,52)cm, cropped version]
[67(67,70,70)cm, long version]
Ending on a WS row.
Shape neck Work 35(40,43,48)sts, turn and leave rem 56(61,68,73)sts on a holder. Work each side of neck separately.
Cast off 3 sts at neck edge on next row, then 3 sts on every alt row, 2 times, then dec 1 st at beg of foll alt rows, 2(2,4,4)times.
Shape shoulder Cast off 8(9,10,11)sts at beg of next and foll alt rows. Work 1 row. Cast off rem 8(11,10,13)sts.
With RS facing, leave 21(21,25,25)sts on a holder, rejoin yarn to rem sts and complete second side to match first side, rev all shaping.

BACK

Work Back Bodice to match front bodice, omitting neck shaping and working shoulder shaping into last 6 rows as follows;
Cast off 8(9,10,11)sts at beg of next 4 rows, then 8(11,10,13)sts at beg of next 2 rows. Leave rem 43(43,51,51)sts on a holder.

Stellar - Cropped Sweater, left
Stellar - Long Sweater, previous 2 pages

SLEEVE

Using 3.25mm needles, cast on 64(64,69,69)sts and work in rib as for Back and Front for 6cm, inc 0(0,1,1)sts in last WS row [64(64,70,70)sts]. Change to 4.00mm needles and work 4 rows rev st st. Now refer to sleeve graph (26 row pattern repeat) for texture pattern.

Shape sleeve Inc 1 st at each end of 5th row, 15(15,13,13)times, then 6th(6th,3rd,3rd)row, 5(5,14,14)times [104(104,124,124)sts] [109(109,111,111) rows, excluding band]. Work 6 rows without shaping, adjust length here if desired.

Shape sleeve top Cast off 10 sts at beg of next 2 rows, then 3 sts at beg of every foll row, 6(6,16,16)times, then 2 sts at beg of every foll row, 14(14,4,4)times. Cast off rem 38(38,48,48)sts.

MAKING UP

Press all pieces gently on WS using a warm iron over a damp cloth. Using Backstitch, join shoulder seams. Centre sleeves and join. Join side and sleeve seams using Edge to Edge stitch on ribs.

Neckband With RS facing, using 3.75mm circular needle and col 1, pick up and k 20(20,24,24)sts down left side front neck, 21(21,25,25) sts from holder at centre, 20(20,24,24)sts up right side front neck and 43(43,51,51)sts across back neck [105(105,125,125) sts]. Work 14 rounds in rib as for Back and Front. Cast off in rib. Press seams.

Front & Back Bodice

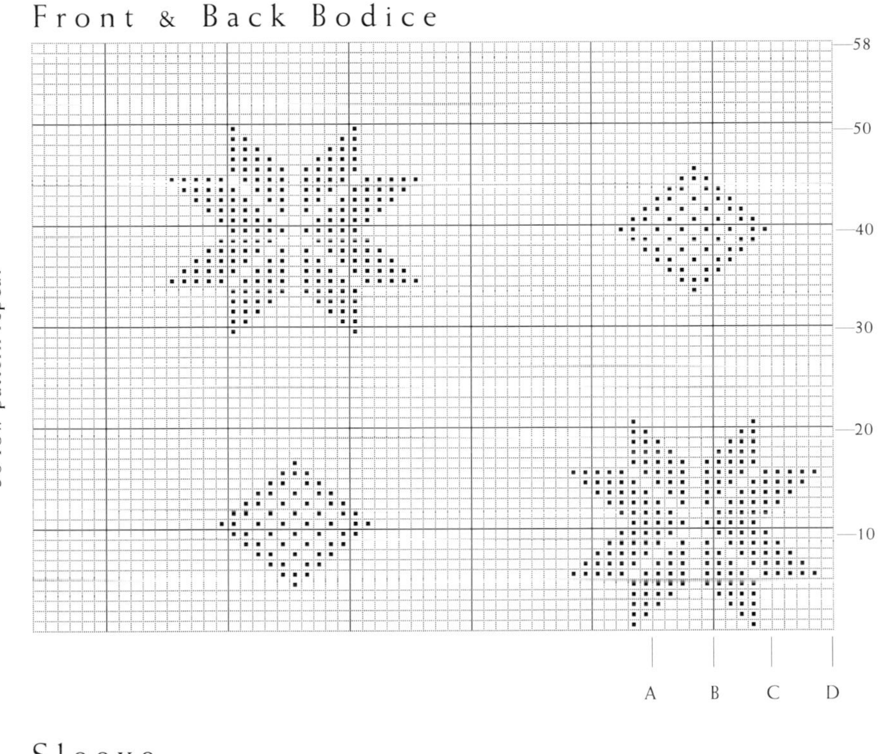

Sleeve

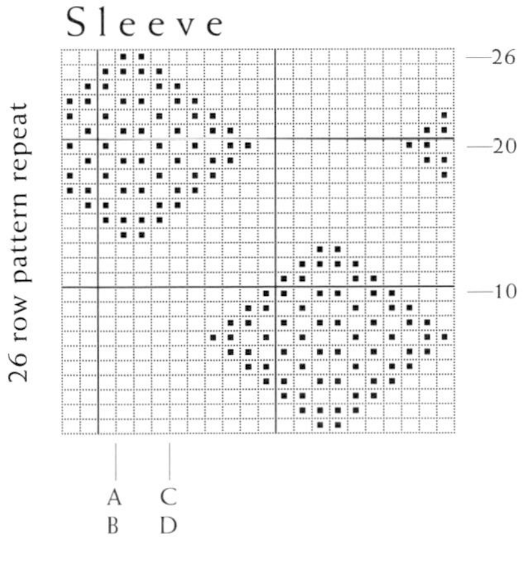

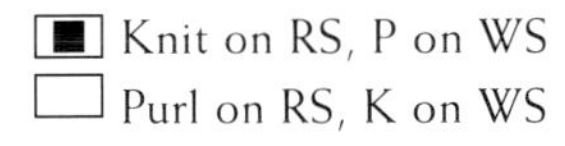

Graph note;
Begin working at position marked for size being knitted and work left. Then work from far right to left in repeat for remainder of row. This row sets position for pattern.

Stellar - Cropped Sweater, left

KASHMIR

MEASUREMENTS

Hat Sizes One Size fits all

Unisex Sweater (left)

Unisex Sizes	A	(B	C	D)	
To fit chest/bust	80-90	90-100	100-110	110-120	cm
Bodice circumference	110	120	130	140	cm
Bodice length	70	70	70	70	cm
Sleeve length	43	43	49	49	cm

Women's Jacket (previous 2 pages)

Sizes	A	(B	C	D)	
To fit bust	80	90	100	110	cm
Bodice circumference	110	120	130	140	cm
Bodice length	72	72	72	72	cm
Sleeve length	47	47	47	47	cm

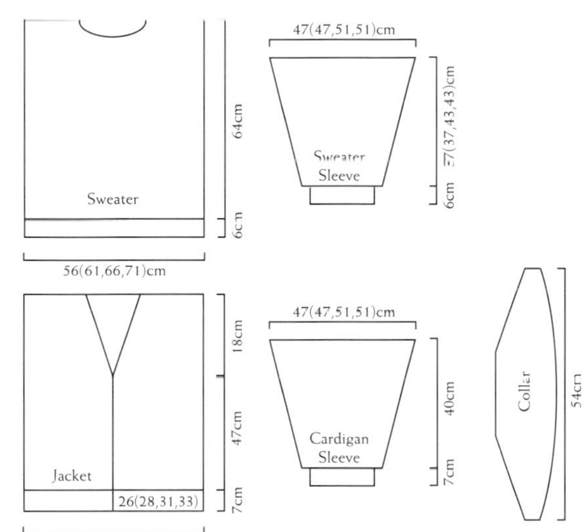

NEEDLES

Sweater

1 pair 3.75mm needles (USA 5) (UK 9)
1 pair 4.00mm needles (USA 6) (UK 8)
3.75mm circular needle (USA 5) (UK9)

Jacket

1 pair 3.25mm needles (USA 3) (UK 10).
1 pair 3.75mm needles (USA 5) (UK 9)
1 pair 4.00mm needles (USA 6) (UK 8)

Hat

1 pair 3.25mm needles (USA 3) (UK 10).
1 pair 4.00mm needles (USA 6) (UK 8)

BUTTONS

Jacket / 5 x 3.5mm buttons (Durango H43 (35)),
See page 106 for Durango Button Company details.

Kashmir - Jacket, previous 2 pages
Kashmir - Sweater, left

YARN

Jo Sharp 8 ply DK Pure Wool Hand Knitting Yarn.

Code	Key	Colour	A	(B	C	D)	
Unisex Sweater							
A	■	Slate 328	9	9	10	11	x 50g balls
B	□	Black 302	5	5	6	6	x 50g balls
C	☒	Ink 901	2	2	2	3	x 50g balls
D	⧄	Owl 801	1	1	1	1	x 50g ball
E	+	Lichen 803	1	2	2	2	x 50g balls
F	O	Embers 804	1	1	1	1	x 50g ball
G	∩	Smoke 339	1	1	1	2	x 50g balls
H	·	Ginger 322	1	1	1	1	x 50g ball
I	♥	Amethyst 503	1	1	1	1	x 50g ball
J	◤	Slate 328	(yarn allocated above)				
K	⁘	Ink 901	(yarn allocated above)				
Women's Jacket							
A	■	Smoke 339	4	4	5	5	x 50g balls
B	□	Ebony 902	11	12	12	12	x 50g balls
C	☒	Embers 804	1	1	1	2	x 50g balls
D	⧄	Winter 904	2	2	2	2	x 50g balls
E	+	Brick 333	1	1	1	1	x 50g ball
F	O	Lichen 803	1	2	2	2	x 50g balls
G	∩	Amethyst 503	3	3	3	3	x 50g balls
H	·	Chartreuse 330	1	1	1	2	x 50g balls
I	♥	Violet 319	1	1	2	2	x 50g balls
J	◤	Ebony 902	(yarn allocated above)				
K	⁘	Amethyst 503	(yarn allocated above)				
Hat							
A		Ebony 902	1 x 50g ball				
B		Lichen 803	1 x 50g ball				

TENSION

22.5 sts and 30 rows measured over 10cm (approx. 4") Stocking Stitch and Intarsia, using 4.00mm needles.

KASHMIR SWEATER

FRONT

Using 3.75mm needles and col A, cast on 126(138,148,160)sts and work 6cm k1, p1 rib, ending on a WS row.

Change to 4.00mm needles. Refer to bodice graph (122 row pattern repeat) for colour changes and working in st st, cont until work measures 57cm (excluding band) ending with a WS row **.

Shape neck Keeping patt correct, work 51(57,62,68)sts, turn and leave rem sts on a holder. Work each side separately. Cast off 2 sts at neck edge on next row and every alt row twice, then 1 st on foll alt rows, 3 times, [42(48,53,59)sts]. Work 11 rows straight. Cast off.

...continue page 82

KASHMIR GRAPH

Sweater & Jacket Bodice
Sweater Sleeve

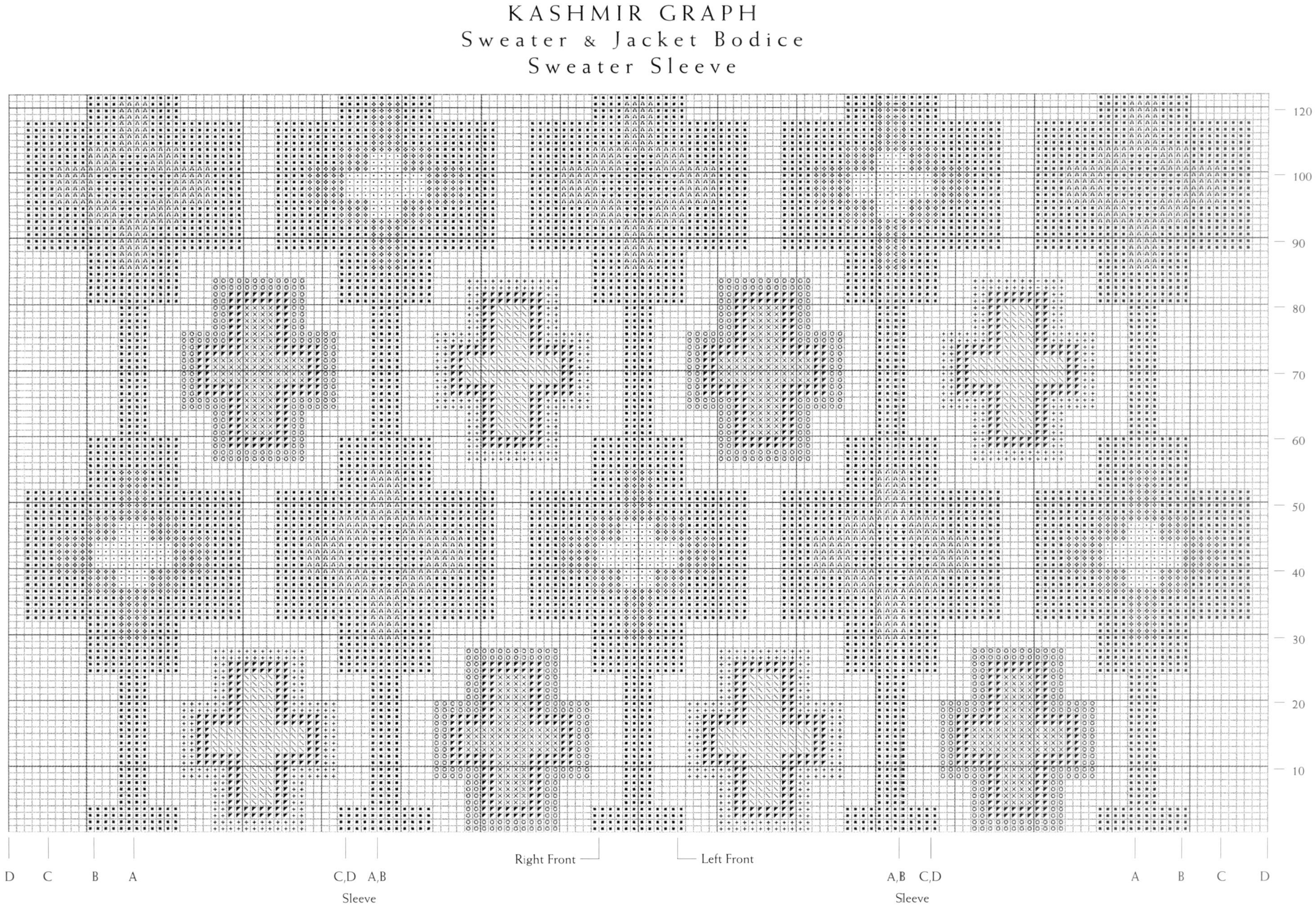

KASHMIR GRAPH
Jacket Sleeve

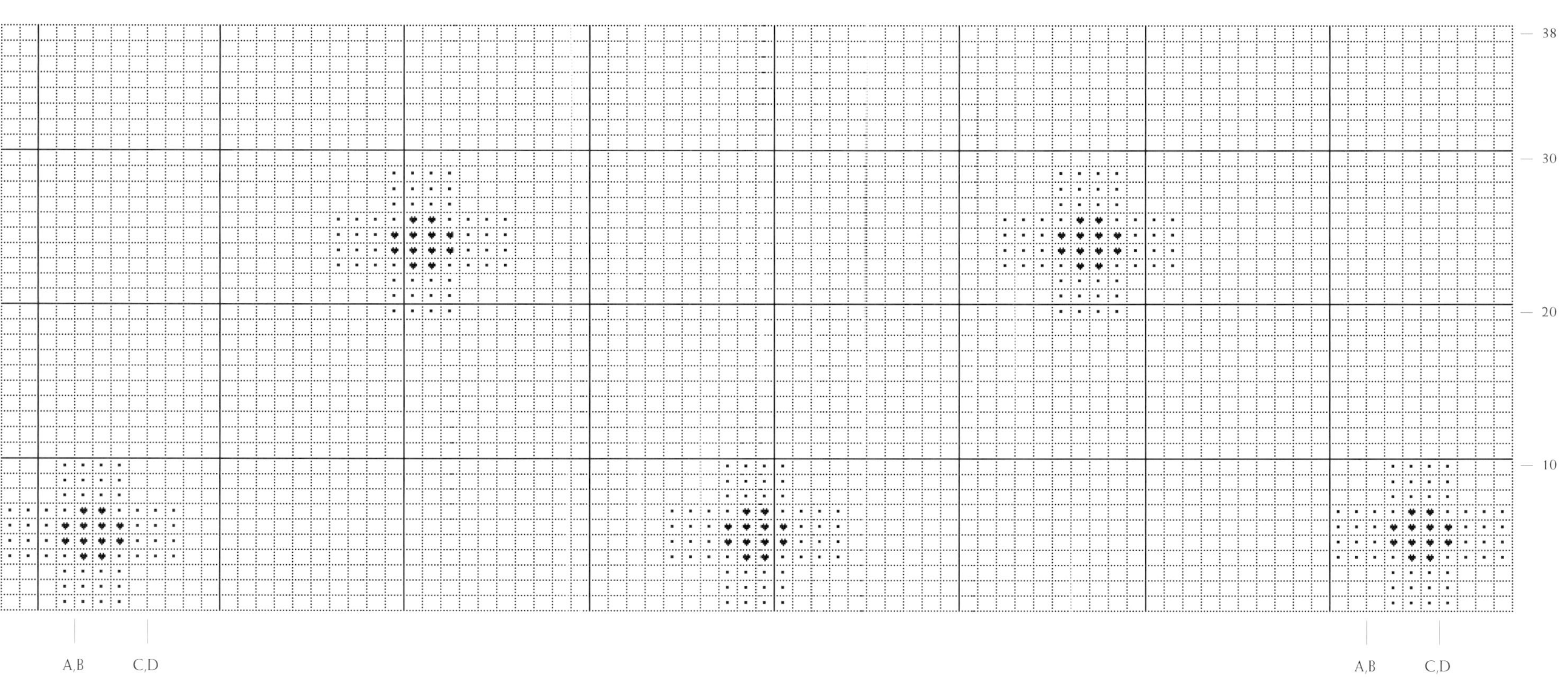

With RS facing, leave 24sts on holder, rejoin yarn to rem sts and complete second side to match first side, rev all shaping.

BACK

Work as for front to **. Cont without shaping until Back bodice length matches Front bodice length. Cast off.

SLEEVES

It is advised, when knitting this unisex garment for a man, to use the size "D" sleeve.

Using 3.75mm needles and col A, cast on 54(54,62,62)sts and work 6cm k1, p1 rib increasing 12 sts evenly across last WS row [66(66,74,74)sts]. Now change to 4.00mm needles and refer to graph (38 row pattern repeat) for colour changes, working in st st;

Shape sleeves Inc 1 st at each end of 7th row, then foll 5(5,6,6)th rows, 19 times [106(106,114,114)sts] [102(102,121,121)rows excluding band].

Work 8(8,9,9) rows straight**. Cast off.

MAKING UP

Press all pieces gently on WS with a warm iron over a damp cloth. Using Backstitch, join shoulder seams. With WS facing, centre sleeves and join. Join side and sleeve seams.

Neck band With RS facing, using 3.75mm circular needle and col A, pick up and k 28 sts down left side front neck, 24 sts from holder at centre, 28 sts up right side front neck and 44 sts across back neck (124 sts). Working in rounds, work 4.5cm in k2, p2 rib. Cast off. Press seams.

KASHMIR JACKET

LEFT FRONT

Using 3.75mm needles and col D, cast on 78(84,90,94)sts and work 2 rows k1, p1 rib.

Cont in rib and colour sequence as follows;

Row 3 Col G

Row 4 Col I

Row 5 & 6 Col B

Row 7 Col F

Row 8 Col G

Repeat rows 1 - 8, once, then 1 - 5 once (21 rows).

Row 22 Col B, working in k1, p1 rib, dec 20(20,21,19)sts evenly across row [58(64,69,75)sts]. Change to 4.00mm needles and working in st st refer to graph for colour changes and patt repeat. Patt until work, excluding band, measures 47cm, ending on a WS row.

Shape neck (RS) Keeping patt correct, dec 1 st at neck edge on next row, then every foll 4th row, 8 times, then on foll alt row, once [48(54,59,65)sts] (35 shaping rows).

Work 19 rows without shaping. Cast off.

RIGHT FRONT

Make Right Front to match Left Front, reversing all shaping.

BACK

Using 3.75mm needles and col D, cast on 156(170,184,198)sts and work in rib to match front band, decreasing 30(32,36,37)sts in last WS row [126(138,148,160)sts].

Change to 4.00mm needles and working in st st, refer to graph for col changes and patt repeat. Patt until back length matches Front length, incorporating back neck shaping into last 6 rows as follows;

(RS) Patt 56(62,67,73)sts, turn and leave rem 70(76,81,87)sts on a holder. Work each side of neck separately. Cast off 4 sts at beg of next WS row, then 4 sts on foll alt row, work 2 rows, cast off rem [48(54,59,65)sts]. Rejoin yarn to rem sts and cast off centre 14sts. Work second side to match first side, reversing all shaping.

SLEEVES

Using 3.25mm needles and col B, cast on 54(54,62,62)sts and work 7cm in k1, p1 rib, increasing 12 sts evenly across last WS row [66(66,74,74)sts].

Now change to 4.00mm needles and refer to Jacket Sleeve Graph (38 row pattern repeat) and work in st st throughout. Note that colour pattern is worked into sleeve over central 82 sts only

Shape sleeve Inc 1 st at each end of 7th row, then foll 5th rows, 19 times [106(106,114,114)sts] (102 rows excluding band). Work 17 rows straight. (adjust length here if desired). Cast off.

POCKET LININGS

Make 2

Using 4.00mm needles and col B, cast on 36 sts.

Work 63 rows st st. Cast off.

COLLAR

Using 3.75mm needles and Col B, cast on 56sts and work 1 row k1, p1 rib.

Working in colour sequence as for Front Rib, beg with rows 5 - 8, then repeating rows 1 - 8 throughout.

Inc 5 sts at beg of every row, 20 times (156 sts) (21 rows).

Row 22 Rib 50, M1 *rib 7, M1, rep from * 8 times, rib 50.

Row 23 Rib 50 M1 *rib 8, M1, rep rem * 8 times, rib 50 (174 sts).

Rib 7 rows straight.

Change to 4.00mm needles and rib 8 rows.

Cast off in col D.

MAKING UP

Press all pieces (except collar and ribs) gently on WS using a warm iron over a damp cloth. Using Backstitch, join shoulder seams. Centre sleeves and join, join sleeve seam using Edge to Edge on rib.

Place pockets Slip Stitch RS of pocket linings to WS of fronts on 3 sides, placing cast on edge of lining along edge where st st begins, after rib bodice band. Using Backstitch, join side seams, stitching both pocket lining and Front to Back for first 5cm above lower band, then stitch pocket lining only to back for next 14cm, then Fronts to Back for remainder.

Pocket edgings With RS facing, using 3.25mm needles and col B, pick up and K 35 sts evenly along side edge (pocket) opening on Fronts. Work 3 rows k1, p1, rib. Cast off. Slip stitch sides of pocket edgings into position, overlapping back.

Join collar Using Edge to edge stitch, stitch collar piece to neck hole and along shaping edges of left and right front pieces.

Button Band Using 3.25mm needles and colour B, with RS facing, pick up and knit 155 sts evenly along left front from bottom edge to beg of neck shaping. Beginning with row 3 of colour sequence for Front Rib, work 16 rows k1, p1 rib. Cast off evenly in rib. Mark positions for 5 buttons, the first to come 2cm down from beg neck shaping, the last to come 2cm up from bottom edge, the remaining 3 to be spaced evenly between.

Button hole band Work as for button band along right front, making button holes to correspond with position of buttons. Sew the ends of the bands to thecollar. Press seams.

KASHMIR HAT

Using 3.25mm needles and col A, cast on 116 sts and work 2cm st st ending on a WS row. Now work 2cm k2, p2 rib, ending on a WS row.

Change to 4.00mm needles and work 4 rows Garter (knit all rows).

Cont in st st for 6cm, ending on a WS row.

Work 4 rows Garter st.

Change to col B and work 2 rows st st.

Change to col A and work 4 rows Garter st.

Shape crown (RS) K1 [sl1, k1, psso, k15, k2tog] 6 times, k1 (104 sts).

Purl 1 row.

Next row K1, [sl1, k1, psso, k13, k2tog]6 times, k1 (92 sts).

Purl 1 row.

Cont working in st st, dec 12 sts every RS row until 20 sts remain.

Next row (RS) K2 tog across row (10sts).

Break yarn, leaving enough length for sewing. Draw yarn through rem sts and pull tog tightly and sew seam using Backstitch.

Embroider motifs to hat Using Swiss Darning or Duplicate Stitch technique, and col B, work 7 cross motifs (as illustrated) with 6 stitch intervals between, noting first cross to begin 7 sts from seam.

ECLIPSE

MEASUREMENTS

Unisex Sizes	A	(B	C	D)	
To fit chest/bust	80-90	90-100	100-110	110-120	cm
Bodice Circumference	96	106	116	126	cm
Bodice Length	61	61	63	66	cm

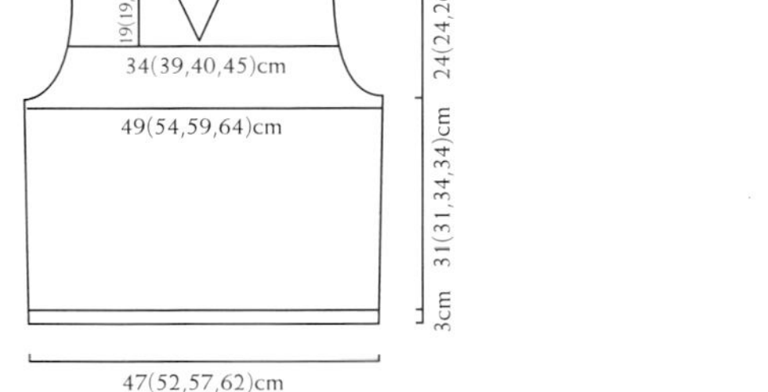

YARN

Jo Sharp 8 ply DK Pure Wool Hand Knitting Yarn

Colour	Yarn Quantity				
Unisex sizes	A	(B	C	D)	
Smoke 339	7	7	8	8	x 50g balls

NEEDLES

1 pair 4.50mm needles (USA 7) (UK 7)
1 pair 4.00mm needles (USA 6) (UK 8)
1 pair 3.25mm needles (USA 3) (UK 10)
1 set 4.00mm circlar nedles (USA 6) (UK 8)

TENSION

19.5sts and 26 rows measured over 10cm (approx. 4") Stocking Stitch, using 4.5mm needles.

FRONT

Using 4.00mm needles, cast on 92(102,112,122)sts and work 10 rows k2, p2 rib, dec 1 st in last WS row [91(101,111,121)sts].
Change to 4.50mm needles and cont in st st.
Work 72(72,82,82)rows [28(28,28,31)cm excluding band].
Inc 1 st at each end of next row, then foll alt row, once [95(105,115,125)sts].
Work 5 rows without shaping [80(80,80,90)rows].
Shape armholes (RS) Cast off 4(4,8,8)sts at beg of next 2 rows. Then dec 1 st at each end of next row, then every foll row, 4 times, then on every alt row, 5 times [67(77,79,89)sts] [97(97,97,107)rows].
Work 3 rows without shaping
Shape neck (RS) Work 33(38,39,44)sts, turn and leave rem 34(39,40,45)sts on a holder. Work each side of neck separately. Keeping armhole edge straight, dec 1 st at neck edge on next WS row, then on foll row, then on every alt row 7(7,6,6)times, then on every 3rd row, 6(6,9,9)times [18(23,22,27)sts] [135(135,142,152)rows]. Work7(7,6,6)rows without shaping [142(142,148,158)rows].
Shape shoulder (RS) Cast off 3(4,4,5)sts at beg of next row, then 4(5,5,6)sts on foll alt row, three times.
Work 1 row. Cast off rem 3(4,3,4)sts [150(150,156,166)rows excluding band].
Rejoin yarn to rem sts and cast off centre st.
Work second side to match first side, reversing all shaping.

BACK

Work Back bodice to match Front bodice, excluding neck shaping. Shape shoulders and back neck on last 8 rows as follows;
Row 143(143,149,159) (RS) Cast off 3(4,4,5)sts at beg of next 2 rows, then 4(5,5,6)sts at beg next RS row. Work 20(23,22,25)sts, turn and leave rem 37(41,44,48)sts on a holder.
Work each side of back neck separately.
Cast off 5 sts at neck edge on next row, then 4(5,5,6)sts at beg next row, then 4sts at neck edge, then 4(5,5,6)sts on next row.
Work 1 row. Cast off rem 3(4,3,4)sts.
Join yarn to rem sts and cast off 13(13,17,17)sts.
Work second side to match first side reversing all shaping.

MAKING UP

Press all pieces gently on WS using a warm iron over a damp cloth. With RS facing, using Backstitch, join shoulder seams.
Armhole bands With RS facing, Using 3.25mm needles, pick up and k 120(120,130,130)sts evenly around armhole edge. Work 8 rows k2, p2, rib.
Cast off in rib. Using Backstitch, join side and armhole band seams.
Neckband With RS facing, using 4.00mm circular needles, beginning at centre front, pick up and knit 52(52,62,62)sts up right front neck,32(32,36,36)sts across back neck and 52(52,62,62)sts down left front neck. Now working back and forth in rows;
Row 1 (WS) Purl.
Row 2 Knit.
Row 3 Purl.
Row 4 Purl.
Row 5 Knit.
Cast off knitwise.
Sew neckband ends into position, overlapping at centre front. Press Seams.

Eclipse - Unisex Vest, left & previous 2 pages

ORIOLE

ORIOLE

MEASUREMENTS

Unisex Sizes	A	(B	C	D)	
To fit chest/bust	80-90	90-100	100-110	110-120	cm
Bodice Circumference	102	106	122	132	cm
Bodice length (cropped)	51	51	54	54	cm
Bodice length (classic)	66	66	69	69	cm

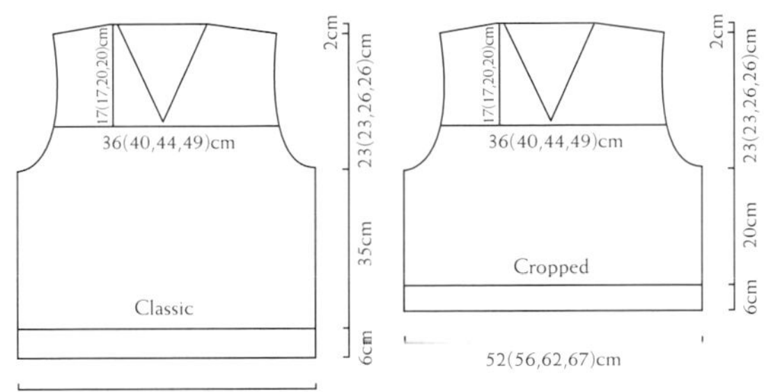

YARN

Jo Sharp 8ply DK Pure Wool Hand Knitting Yarn

Code	Key	Colour	A	(B	C	D)	Yarn Quantity
Cropped vest							
	+	Cape 508	1	1	2	2	x 50g balls
	O	Citrus 509	1	1	2	2	x 50g balls
	■	Ink 901	1	1	2	2	x 50g balls
A	□	Heron 802	5	5	6	6	x 50g balls
Classic Vest							
	+	Orchard 906	1	2	2	2	x 50g balls
A	O	Ebony 902	6	7	7	7	x 50g balls
	■	Silk 903	1	2	2	2	x 50g balls
	□	Owl 801	1	2	2	2	x 50g balls

NEEDLES

1 pair 3.25mm (USA 3) (UK 10)
1 pair 4.00mm (USA 6) (UK 8)
1 pair 4.50mm (USA 7) (UK 7)

Oriole - Classic Vest, left & right
Oriole - Cropped Vest, previous 2 pages

TENSION

Fairisle; 24 stitches and 26 rows measured over 10cm (approx. 4") using 4.50mm needles.
Stocking Stitch; 22.5 stitches and 30 rows measured over 10cm (approx. 4") using 4.00mm needles.

FRONT

Using 3.25mm needles and Col A cast on 112(122,136,148)sts. Work in k1, p1 rib for 6 cms inc 14 sts evenly across last row [127(137,151,163)sts]. Change to 4.50mm needles. Refer to Graph (17 row pattern repeat) and work (20cm cropped vest or 35cm classic vest, excluding band) ending on a WS row.
Armhole shaping Keeping patt correct cast off 7(7,8,8) sts at beg of next 4 rows. Dec 1st at each end of next row, then foll alt rows, 5 times. [87(97,107,119)sts].
Next Row Work 43(48,53,59,)sts turn and leave rem 44(49,54,60)sts on holder. Work each side of neck separately.
Shape V neck Cont on these 43(48,53,59)sts keeping armhole edge straight dec 1st at neck edge on next row then every alt row 19(19,22,22)times. Work 1(1,3,3) rows straight.
Shoulder shaping (RS) Cast off 7(9,9,12)sts at beg of next row and foll alt row once, then cast off rem 9(10,12,12)sts.
With RS facing, slip next stitch onto a thread and leave. Rejoin yarn to rem sts, and work second side to match first side, rev all shaping.

BACK

Using 3.25mm needles, and Col A cast on 118(126,138,150)sts work in k1, p1 rib for 6cms. Change to 4.00mm needles. Working in st st, work (20cm for cropped vest or 35cm for classic vest, excluding band) ending on a WS row.

Armhole shaping (RS) Cast off 5(5,6,6)sts at beg of next 4 rows, then dec 1 st each end of foll alt rows, 8 times [82(90,98,110)sts] Work straight until armhole edge measures 23(23,26,26)cms from beg of shaping.

Shape shoulder and back neck together Next Row (RS) Cast off 7(8,9,11)sts, work 26(29,30,34)sts, turn and leave rem 49(53,59,65)sts on a holder. Work each side of neck separately.

Cast off 6 sts at beg (neck edge) on next row, then 7(8,9,11)sts at beg next row, then 6 sts at beg (neck edge) of next row, work to end of row. Cast off rem 7(9,9,11)sts.

Rejoin yarn to rem sts and cast off 16(16,20,20) centre sts, then work second side to match first side, reversing all shaping.

MAKING UP

Press all pieces gently on WS using a warm iron over a damp cloth. Using Backstitch, join right shoulder seam.

Neckband With RS facing, using 3.25mm needles and col A, pick up and k 54(54,66,66)sts evenly along left side of front neck, knit centre st from thread, pick up and k54(54,66,66)sts evenly along right side of front neck, then pick up and knit 40(40,44,44)sts across back neck [148(148,176,176)sts].

Row 1 *K1, p1; rep from * to end

Row 2 Rib to within 2 sts of centre st, yb, sl 1, k1, psso, k1 (centre st), k2 tog, rib to end.

Row 3 Rib to within 2 sts of centre st, k2tog, p1, k2tog tbl, rib to end.

Repeat Rows 2 & 3, 4 times (11 rows rib in all).

Cast off in rib.

Using Backstitch join left shoulder and neckband seam.

Armhole bands With RS facing, using 3.25mm needles and col A, pick up and k125(125,135,135)sts evenly along armhole edge.

Work 7 rows, k1, p1 rib.Cast off loosely in rib.

Join side seams and armhole band seams. Press seams.

Oriole - Cropped Vest, above.

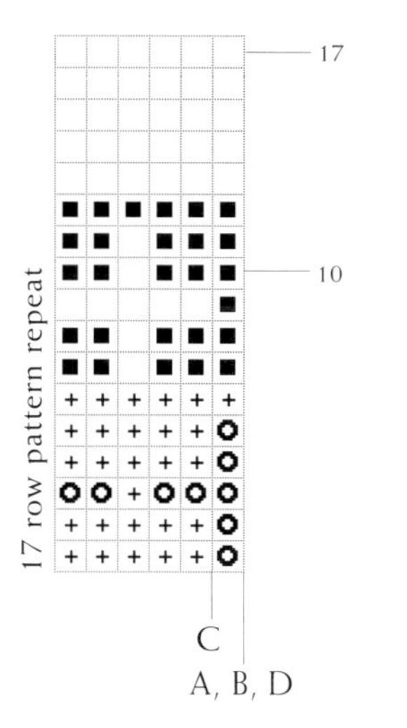

Graph note; Begin working at position marked for size being knitted and work left. Then work from far right to left in repeat for remainder of row.

This row sets position for pattern.

Oriole - Classic Vest, right

HEATHER

MEASUREMENTS

Sizes	A	(B	C	D)	
To fit bust	80	90	100	110	cm
Bodice circumference	102	110	120	130	cm
Bodice length	64	64	64	64	cm
Sleeve seam length	44	44	44	44	cm

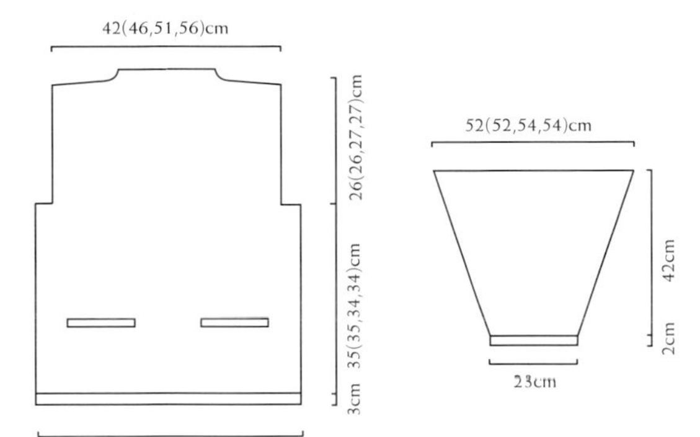

YARN

Jo Sharp 8ply DK Pure Wool Hand Knitting Yarn

Code	Colour	Yarn Quantity				
Sizes		A	(B	C	D)	
Version 1						
A	Hull 705	16	17	17	18	x 50g balls
B	Owl 801	2	2	2	2	x 50g balls
Version 2						
A	Haze 701	16	17	17	18	x 50g balls
B	Ebony 902	2	2	2	2	x 50g balls

NEEDLES

1 pair 3.25mm (USA 3) (UK 10)
1 pair 3.75mm (USA 5) (UK 9)
1 pair 4.00mm (USA 6) (UK 8)

TENSION

24 sts and 36 rows measured over 10cm (approx. 4") Texture Pattern, using 4.00mm needles.

TEXTURE PATTERN

Multiple 4 + 3
Row 1 (RS) Knit
Row 2 K3, *p1, k3 rep from * to end.
Row 3 & 4 Rep the last 2 rows once.
Row 5 Knit.
Row 6 K1, p1 * k3, p1; rep from * to last st, k1.
Row 7 & 8 Rep the last 2 rows once.
Rep these 8 rows.

Heather - Version 2, left
Heather - Version 1, previous 2 pages

POCKET LINING (make 2)

Using 4.00mm needles and col 1, cast on 46 sts and work 50 rows st st, leave sts on a holder.

FRONT

Note; Although the garment is knit to 64cm, the finished length when worn will drop to 70cm, due to the nature of the stitch & weight of the pockets.

Using 3.25mm needles and col B, cast on 127(135,147,159)sts and work 3 cms in texture patt. Change to 4.00mm needles and working in col A, patt until work measures 21cm (including band) and ending with a WS row.

Place pocket lining Patt 7(10,14,18)sts, slip next 46 sts onto holder and in place of these, pick up 46 sts from pocket lining stitch holder and patt across these sts, patt 21(23,27,31)sts, slip next 46 sts onto holder and in place of these, pick up 46 sts from pocket lining stitch holder and patt across these sts, patt rem 7(10,14,18)sts.

Cont in patt until work measures 38(38,37,37)cm, ending on a WS row.

Shape armhole Keeping patt correct, cast off 12 sts at beg of next 2 rows [103(111,123,135)sts.

Cont until work measures 26(26,27,27)cm from beg armhole shaping and ending on a WS row.

Shape collar Keeping patt correct, cast off 19(23,26,32)sts at beg of next 2 rows, then 2 sts at beg of foll alt rows, 4 times, then dec 1 st at beg of foll alt rows, twice [55(55,61,61)sts]. Work 8 rows without shaping. Cast off.

BACK

Work as for front, omitting pockets.

SLEEVES

Using 3.25mm needles and col B, cast on 55(55,59,59)sts and work 8 rows in Texture patt. Change to 4.00mm needles and col A, patt 4 rows.

Shape sleeve (RS) Keeping patt correct, inc 1 st at each end of next row, then every foll 4th row, 23 times, then every foll 3rd row, 12 times. [127(127,131,131)sts] (141 rows). Work 17 rows without shaping, adjust length here if desired.
Cast off.

MAKING UP

Using Backstitch, join shoulder and collar seams. Centre sleeves and join. Join side and sleeve seams.

Pocket tops With RS facing, using 3.75mm needles and col B, work 1 row in texture patt across sts left on st holder. Change to 3.25mm needles cont in patt for 4 rows. Cast off. Sew pocket linings in place on WS and finish off pocket tops on RS.

JO SHARP

HOW TO CARE FOR YOUR PURE WOOL KNITWEAR

Investment knitting

With care the Jo Sharp garment you create this year will become a trusted favourite in the years to come. Spun from premium grade long fibre fleece, Jo Sharp yarn knits into a hard-wearing item of clothing that is beautifully warm and soft. It is not surprising that Jo's wool performs so well when you consider it has survived all the elements while still on the sheep's back. Pure wool is practical, long-lasting and natural. A Jo Sharp wool garment will stand up to harsh outdoor conditions whilst keeping its softness and good looks throughout years of wear.
Wool knitwear requires care and attention when it is washed, however it does not soil easily and requires maintenance less frequently than other fibres.

Not machine wash treated

Jo Sharp Hand Knitting Yarn has a natural crimp and elasticity which makes it satisfying to knit with. Its waxy outer coating of tiny overlapping scales, (rather like roof shingles) repels liquids and particles of dust or dirt. Wool contains millions of tiny pockets of air which act as natural thermal insulators. Unfortunately, machine wash treatment puts an artificial resin coating on wool fibres, effectively gluing them together and damaging natural thermal characteristics. This treatment also gives wool yarn an unnatural shiny appearance. For these reasons, Jo Sharp chose not to machine wash treat her yarn.

Less pilling

Inferior short fibres (which can cause pilling and itching) are removed during processing of Jo Sharp yarn. This treatment improves the yarn's natural softness and wash and wear performance. With care, your quality Jo Sharp garment will improve with age and wear.

What causes wool knitwear to shrink?

Nature designed wool fibres to be a protective coating for sheep in all weather. The unique outer scale structure of the wool fibre resists soiling, but is also the reason why wool shrinks when not cared for properly. With severe agitation or tumble drying, the scales on the fibre lock together causing the garment to reduce in size and become thick and fluffy (felted). If you carefully follow the washing instructions on the inside of the Jo Sharp yarn label and at right, you should not encounter any problems with shrinkage.

Hand washing

For the best result, turn garment inside out and gently hand wash in lukewarm water, using a wool detergent. Rinse thoroughly in lukewarm water. Rinse again in cold water.

Drying

To remove excess moisture after washing, roll garment inside a large towel and gently squeeze or, alternatively, spin dry inside a pillow case. Never tumble dry. Place garment on a flat surface in the shade to dry, coaxing it back into shape whilst damp. Drying flat is recommended.
Do not dry directly in front of an open or artificial fire.

Machine washing

If care is taken, a Jo Sharp wool garment may be successfully machine washed. Turn the garment inside out and place inside a sealed pillow slip (sew pillow closed or use a special casing for wool washing that zips closed). Use a wool detergent and a gentle cycle with a medium spin and lukewarm water. Any severe agitation may shrink your garment. Dry as above.

Dry cleaning

Generally is not recommended as residual dry cleaning chemicals tend to harden wool fabric.

Combing

When our extra long fibre yarn is processed, most of the short fibres are removed. If, in the first few weeks of wear, a few remaining short fibres shed, causing a small amount of pilling, these pills should be combed from your garment using a "de-piller" comb. De-pilling combs are generally inexpensive and are available from craft and knitting stores.

Yarn specification

Jo Sharp 8ply DK Pure Wool Hand Knitting Yarn is made from extra fine and soft 100% Merino/Border Leicester fleece. (DK is the USA and UK equivalent of Australian 8 ply) One Ball of yarn is 50g (1 3/4 oz) and approx. 98 Mtrs (107 yards) in length.
Tension/Gauge: 22.5 sts and 30 rows, measured over 10cm (approx 4") of Stocking Stitch and using 4.00 mm (UK 8) (USA 6) needles.

339 Smoke
504 Aegean
336 Mosaic
508 Cape
304 Coral
309 Cherry
316 Jade
509 Citrus
319 Violet
503 Amethyst
505 Plum
330 Chartreuse
312 Renaissance
333 Brick
313 Olive
332 Terracotta
507 Miro
506 Chestnut
320 Gold
902 Ebony
904 Winter
901 Ink
001 Summer
002 Pistachio
004 Dijon
003 Tangerine

324 Lilac
323 Antique
322 Ginger
326 Ruby
307 Wine
318 Forest
327 Navy
325 Mulberry
502 Eucalypt
302 Black
328 Slate
705 Hull
706 Storm
704 Monsoon
703 Ivory
701 Haze
301 Natural
335 Linen
329 Khaki
337 Avocado
803 Lichen
801 Owl
802 Heron
804 Embers
906 Orchard
903 Silk

The shades represented above are more closely accurate than those illustrated in the locational photographs in this book, however, it is advisable to purchase a Jo Sharp yarn sample card for completely accurate yarn shade reference

JO SHARP

Hand Knitting Collection Stockists

AUSTRALIA

Head Office & Mail Order Enquiries
JO SHARP HAND KNITTING YARN
PO Box 357 Albany WA 6331
Australia
Telephone +61 08 9842 2250
Facsimile +61 08 9842 2260
email - yarn@josharp.com.au
website - www.josharp.com.au

Australian Retail Stores Enquiries
Coats Spencer Crafts
Private Bag 15, Mulgrave North
Victoria Australia 3170
Telephone 03 9561 2288
Facsimile 03 9561 2298
Toll Free Orders 1800 641 277
Toll Free Enquiries 1800 801 195

New South Wales

Armidale Wool Shop	Armidale	02 6772 7083
Champion Textiles	Newtown	02 9519 6677
Cherry Hill	Pennant Hills	02 9484 0212
Greta's Handcraft Centre	Lindfield	02 9416 2489
Hornsby Wool & Craft Nook	Hornsby	02 9482 4924
Inca Wool Shed	Turramurra	02 9440 9111
Jimana Crafts	Long Jety	02 4332 1307
Knit It	Beecroft	02 9875 5844
Pins & Needles	Merimbula	02 6495 3646
Tapestry Crafts	Sydney	02 9299 3470
The Calico Connection	Wentworth Falls	02 4757 1352
Wool Inn	Penrith	02 4732 2201
Grace Bros.	North Ryde	02 9887 0122

Australian Capital Territory

Shearing Shed	Manuka	02 6295 0061
Stitch 'n' Time	Mawson	02 6286 4378

Queensland

Miller & Coates	Ascot	07 3268 3955

Tasmania

Knitters of Australia	Moonah	03 6229 6052
Needle & Thread	Devonport	03 6424 6920
The Spinning Wheel	Hobart	03 6234 1711

South Australia

Highgate Needle Nook	Highgate	08 8271 4670
Midway Fabrics	Port Lincoln	08 8682 2641
Pee Jays	Ingle Farm	08 8264 8515
Kadina Craft Centre	Kadina	08 8821 2409

Victoria

Frith MJ & EA	Colac	03 5231 3252
Knight's Habby	Kyabram	03 5852 2862
Knitters of Australia	Hampton	03 9533 1233
Knitters of Australia	Surrey Hills	03 9836 9614
Mooroolbark Craft & Habby	Mooroolbark	03 9726 7291
Myer	Melbourne	03 9661 1111
The Stitchery	Essendon	03 9379 9790
Warrnambool Wool & Uniforms	Warrnambool	03 5562 9599

Western Australia

Boolah Art & Craft Supplies	Albany	08 9842 1042
Crossway's Wool & Fabrics	Subiaco	08 9381 4286
www: woolshop.com.au		
Myer	Perth	08 9221 3444

NEW ZEALAND

Mail Order Enquiries
Knit-A-Holics Unlimited
PO Box 45083
Epuni Railway
Lower Hutt, NZ
Telephone 04 567 4085
Facsimile 04 567 4094
email: knitting@xtra.co.nz

Creative Fashion Centres	Lower Hutt	04 566 4689
	Tawa	04 232 8088
	Hamilton	07 838 3868
Knit World	Auckland	09 837 6111
	Palmerston North	06 356 8974
	New Plymouth	06 758 3171
	Christchurch	03 379 2300
	Hastings	06 878 0090
	Tauranga	07 577 0797
	Dunedin	03 477 0400
	Wellington	04 385 1918
Knit'n'Save	Lower Hutt	04 567 7688
	Levin	06 367 9700
	Paraparaumu	04 298 8756

CANADA

Wholesale Enquiries

Estelle Designs
Units 65/67 2220 Midland Ave.
Scarborough, Ontario M1P 3E6
Telephone 416 298 9922
Facsimile 416 298 2429

Canadian Retail Stores

Alberta	Wool Revival	Edmonton	780 471 2749
British Columbia	Boutique de Laine	Victoria	250 592 9616
	House of Wool	Prince George	604 562 2803
Manitoba	Ram Wools	Winnipeg	204 949 6868
	The Sheep Boutique	Winnipeg	204 786 8887
Ontario	Christina Tandberg Knits	London	519 672 4088
	Elizabeth's Wool Shop	Kitchener	519 744 1881
	Imagiknit 2000	Kilworthy	800 318 9426
	Knit or Knot	Aurora	905 713 1818
	Knit, Sew One	Peterborough	705 745 8588
	London Yarns & Machines	London	519 474 0403
	Muskoka Yarn Connection	Bracebridge	705 645 5819
	Needles and Knits	Aurora	905 713 2066
	Passionknit Ltd	Toronto	416 322 0688
	Romni Wools	Toronto	416 703 0202
	The Needle Emporium	Ancaster	905 648 1994
	The Yarn Tree	Streetsville	905 821 3170
	Village Yarns	Toronto	416 232 2361
	Wool-Tyme	Carlingwood	613 798 0809
	Wool-Tyme	Nepean	613 225 WOOL
Saskatchewan	The Wool Emporium	Saskatoon	306 374 7848

U.S.A.

Wholesale Enquiries

Classic Elite Yarns
300A Jackson Street Lowell, MA 01852
Telephone 978 453 2837
Facsimile 978 452 3085

U.S.A. Retail Stores

Alabama	Yarn Expressions	Huntsville	800-283-8409	
Arizona	Red Rock Knit Shop	Sedona	520-204-1505	www.theshoppingsite.com/redrockneedlepoint/
	Purl's II	Tucson	520-797-8118	
California	Navarro River Knits	Ft. Bragg	707-964-9665	
	BB's Knits	Santa Barbara	805-569-0531	
	In Sheep's Clothing	Davis	530-759-9276	www.insheepsclothing.com
	Knitting in LaJolla	LaJolla	858-456-4687	
	The Black Sheep	Encinitas	760-436-9973	
	Velona's	Anaheim Hills	714-974-1570	
	L'Atelier	Redondo Beach	310-540-4440	
	L'Atelier	Santa Monica	310-394-4665	
	In Stitches	Santa Barbara	805-962-9343	

Hand Knitting Collection Stockists
(continued)

State	Stockist	City	Phone	Website
	Uncommon Threads	Los Altos	650-941-1815	
	Greenwich Yarns	San Francisco	415-567-2535	www.citysearch.com/sfo/greenwichyarn
	Filati Fine Yarns	Danville	925-820-6614	
	Fabrications	Auburn	530-887-0600	www.fabrications-gv.com
	Calistoga Yarns	Calistoga	707-942-5108	
	Knitting Basket	Oakland	510-339-6295	
Connecticut	Wool Connection	Avon	800-933-9665	www.woolconnection.com
	Fabric Place	Cromwell	860-632-5744	www.fabricplace.com
	The Yarn Barn	Woodbridge	203-389-5117	
	Hook & Needles	Westport	800-960-4404	www.hook-n-needle.com
Delaware	Not Just Needlepoint	Wilmington	302-426-1244	
Idaho	Isabel's	Ketchum	208-725-0408	
	Ewe K Knits Ltd/ House of Needlecraft	CoeurD'Alene	888-775-5648	www.ewekknit.com
Illinois	Mosaic Yarn Studio	Des Plaines	847-390-1013	www.mosaicyarnstudio.com
	The Village Knit Whiz	Glenview	847-998-9772	
	Basket of Stitches	Palatine	847-991-5515	
	Fine Line	St. Charles	630-584-9443	
	Barkim Ltd.	Chicago	888-548-2211	www.barkim.com
	The Weaving Workshop	Chicago	773-929-5776	
	Nancy's Knitworks	Springfield	800-676-9813	
	We'll Keep You in Stitches	Chicago	312-642-2540	
Indiana	Sheep's Clothing Supply	Valparaiso	219-462-4300	
	Yarns Unlimited	Bloomington	812-334-2464	
	Mass Ave Knit Shop	Indianapolis	800-675-8565	
Kentucky	Hand Knitters, Ltd	Louisville	502-254-9276	
Massachusettes	Knitting Treasures	Plymouth	508-747-2500	
	Barehill Studios	Harvard	978-456-8669	
	KnitWits	Brookfield	1-877-877-knit (5648)	www.knitwitts.com
	Northampton Wools	Northampton	413-586-4331	
	Colorful Stitches	Lenox	800-413-6111	www.colorful-stitches.com
	I'm in Stitches	Newburyport	978-465-2929	
	Woolcott and Co.	Cambridge	617-547-2837	
	Wild & Woolly Studio	Lexington Ctr.	781-861-7717	
	Snow Goose	Milton	617-698-1190	
	Creative Warehouse	Needham	781-444-9341	
	Ladybug Knitting Shop	Dennis	508-385-2662	www.ladybugknitting.com
	Needle Arts of Concord	Concord	978-371-0424	
Maryland	Woolworks	Baltimore	410-337-9030	
	Yarn Garden of Annapolis	Annapolis	800-738-9276	
Maine	Ardith Keef Gifts	Scarborough	207-883-8689	
	Stitchery Square	Camden	207-236-9773	www.stitching.com/stitcherysquare
Michigan	Yarn Quest	Traverse City	616-929-4277	
	Right Off the Sheep	Birmingham	248-646-7595	
	The Wool & The Floss	Grosse Pointe	313-882-9110	
	Threadbender	Grand Rapids	888-531-6642	www.threadbender.com
	Knitting Room	Birmingham	248-540-3623	
	Whipple Tree Yarn & Gifts	Hudsonville	616-669-4487	
	Stitching Memories	Portage	616-552-9276	
Missouri	Thread Peddler	Springfield	417-886-5404	
	Hearthstone Knits	St. Louis	314-849-9276	
	Lynn's Stitchin Tyme	Marshfield	417-859-4494	
Minnesota	Linden Hills Yarns	Minneapolis	612-929-1255	
	A Sheepy Yarn Shoppe	White Bear Lake	800-480-5462	
	Three Kittens Yarns Shop	St. Paul	800-489-4969	
	Zandy's Yarn Etc.	Burnsville	612-890-3087	
	Skeins	Minnetonka	612-939-4166	
	Needlework Unlimited	Minneapolis	612-925-2454	
North Carolina	Great Yarns	Raleigh	919-832-3599	
Nebraska	Personal Threads Boutique	Omaha	402-391-7733	www.personalthreads.com
New Hampshire	Keepsake Yarnworks	Centre Harbor	603-253-4725	
	The Elegant Ewe	Concord	603-226-0066	

	Charlotte's Web	Exeter	888-244-6460	
New Jersey	The Knitting Gallery	Colts Neck	732-294-9276	
	Simply Knit	Lambertville	609-397-7101	
	Knitters Workshop	Garwood	908-789-1333	
	Accents on Knits	Morristown	973-829-9944	
	Stitching Bee	Chatham	973-635-6691	
New Mexico	Village Wools	Albuquerque	800-766-4553	www.villagewools.com
	The Needle's Eye	Santa Fe	800-883-0706	
New York	The Knitting Corner	Huntington	516-421-2660	
	Happiknits	Commack	516-462-5558	
	The Knitting Place, Inc.	Port Washington	516-944-9276	
	Elegant Needles	Skaneateles	315-685-9276	
	The Yarn Connection	New York	212-684-5099	www.nytoday.com/yarnconnection
	Lee's Yarn Center	Bedford Hills	914-244-3400	
	Heartmade (mail order only)	Brooklyn	800-898-4290	
	Patternworks	Poughkeepsie	800-438-5464	www.patternworks.com
	Village Yarn Shop	Rochester	716-454-6064	
	The Knitting Connection	East Syracuse	351-445-2911	
	The Woolly Lamb	East Aurora	716-655-1911	
	Amazing Threads	Lake Katrine	914-336-5322	
	Sew Brooklyn	Brooklyn	718-499-7383	
Ohio	Wolfe Fibre Arts	Columbus	614-487-9980	
	Fifth Stitch	Defiance	419-782-0991	
Oklahoma	Sealed with a Kiss	Guthrie	405-282-8649	www.swakknit.com
	Mary Jane's	Oklahoma City	405-848-0233	
	Needlework Creations	Tulsa	918-742-0448	
Oregon	Woodland Woolworks	Yamhill	503-662-3641	
	Fiber Nook & Crannys	Corvallis	541-754-8637	
	Northwest Peddlers	Eugene	800-764-9276	www.nwpeddlers.com
	The Web-sters	Ashland	800-482-9801	
Pennsylvania	Kathy's Kreations	Ligonier	724-238-9320	www.kathys-kreations.com
	Mannings Creative	E. Berlin	800-233-7166	www.the-mannings.com
	Oh Susanna Yarns	Lancaster	717-393-5146	
	A Garden of Yarn	Chaddsford	610-459-5599	www.yarngarden.com
	Wool Gathering	Kennett Square	610-444-8236	www.woolgathering.com
Rhode Island	A Stitch Above	Providence	800-949-5648	
Tennesee	Angel Hair Yarns	Nashville	615-269-8833	www.angelhairyarn.com
	Genuine Purl Too	Chattanooga	423 267 7335	
	Knit & Purl	Knoxville	423-690-9983	
Texas	Needleart	Spring	281-288-0585	
	Woolie Ewe	Plano	972-424-3163	
	Turrentines	Houston	713-661-9411	
	Yarn Barn of San Antonio	San Antonio	210-826-3679	
	Donna's Yarn Barn	Austin	512-452-2681	
Utah	Needlepoint Joint	Ogden	801-394-4355	www.needlepointjoint.com
Virginia	Hunt Country Yarns	Middleburg	540-687-5129	
	Aylin's Woolgatherer	Falls Church	703-573-1900	
	Wooly Knits	Mclean	703-448-9665	www.woolyknits.com
	Old Town Needlecrafts	Manassas	703-330-1846	
	Knitting Basket Ltd	Richmond	804-282-2909	
	Orchardside Yarn Shop	Raphine	540-348-5220	
	The Knitting Corner, Inc.	Virginia Beach	757-420-7547	
	On Pins & Needles	Toano	800-484-5191 ext. 9334	
Washington	The Weaving Works	Seattle	888-524-1221	
	Tricoter	Seattle	206-328-6505	
	Lauren's Wild & Wooly	Poulsbo	360-779-3222	
Wisconsin	Jane's Knitting Hutch	Appleton	920-954-9001	www.angelfire.com/biz2/yarnshop/index.html
	Easy Stitchin' Needleart, Inc.	Sister Bay	920-854-2840	
	Ruhama's Yarn & Needlepoint	Milwaukee	414-332-2660	
	Herrschners Inc.	Stevens Point	1-800-713-1239	
	Lakeside Fibers	Madison	608-257-2999	

JO SHARP

Hand Knitting Collection Publications

Knitting Bazaar

Knitting Bazaar contains many easy to knit, richly coloured designs. A sophisticated collection combining traditional knitting technique and contemporary style.
Soft cover, 108 pages.
Available at book stores and yarn stores.

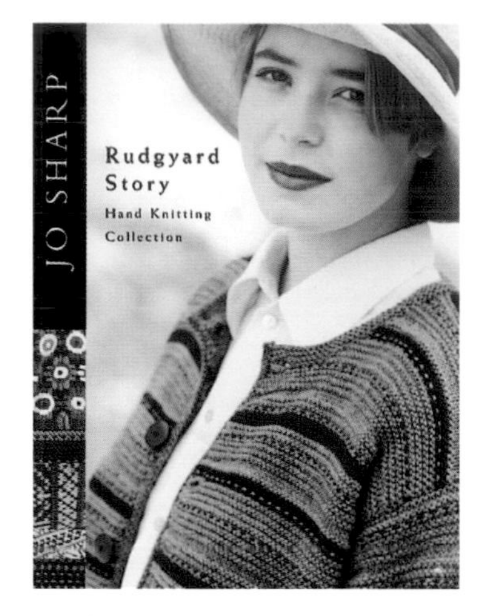

Rudgyard Story Collection

Rudgyard Story is photographed in a beautiful setting in the South west of Australia and is one of the most popular books in the Jo Sharp collection.
Soft cover, 112 pages.
Available at book stores and yarn stores.

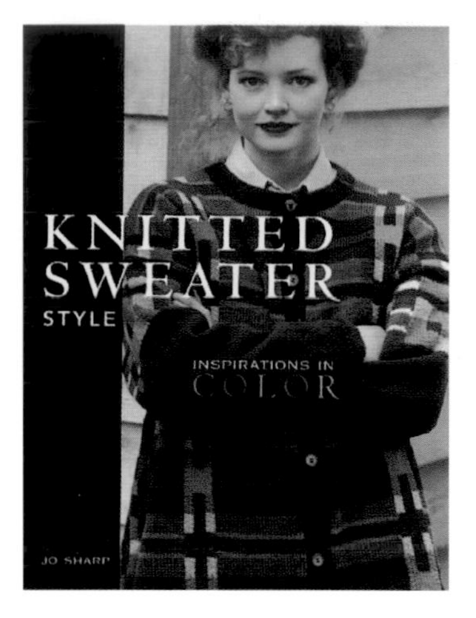

Knitted Sweater Style

A beautiful hard cover colour book for collectors, based around the Jo Sharp individual pattern leaflet collection.
Published by The Taunton Press.
Available at book stores and yarn stores.

West Cape Howe Collection

Projects for knitters at all skill levels. If you have always wanted to design your own multi-colour sweater, you will find a designers blank sweater graph to get you started.
Soft cover, 40 pages.
Available only at yarn stores.

Hanover Bay Collection

This book has a maritime theme and includes patterns for all the family. Projects suitable for knitters at all skill levels.
Soft cover, 48 pages.
Available only at yarn stores.

Yarn Shade Card

Jo Sharp works exclusively with her own shade collection as illustrated on page 101.

The yarn sample card is available by contacting a Jo Sharp yarn stockist as listed on pages 102 to 105.

Buttons

To obtain some of the buttons featured in this book, contact:

The Durango Button Company
1021 C.R. 126
Hesperus, CO. 81326
U.S.A.
phone: 1800-8342001
email: durangobutton@frontier.net

The Jo Sharp Individual Pattern Leaflets (selection featured at right) are available from yarn stores only.

view the complete range, sit a Jo Sharp yarn stockist as listed on pages 102-105 or at www.josharp.com.au.

From left to right

Country Plaid Shirt

Artisan

Fishermans Gansey

Ironbark

Cactus Flower Coat

Rustic Texture Vest

Palms & Camomile

Naples Cardigan

Primitive Birds

Chinese Tapestry

raditional Shawl Collar

Naples Sweater

JO SHARP

Jo Sharp is a knitwear designer of international reputation who lives in a prime wool growing region of Western Australia where she works from her studio overlooking the southern ocean.

Her background in visual arts led her to create her own palette of unique colours and classic knitting designs which have been showcased in several collections.

She shares the photography in her books with her husband with whom she enjoys an idyllic country lifestyle.